LATINO POLITICS IN CALIFORNIA

U.S.–MEXICO CONTEMPORARY PERSPECTIVES SERIES, 10
CENTER FOR U.S.–MEXICAN STUDIES
UNIVERSITY OF CALIFORNIA, SAN DIEGO

Contributors

Rodolfo O. de la Garza
Leo F. Estrada
Patricia Gándara
David G. Gutiérrez
Carole J. Uhlaner
Aníbal Yáñez-Chávez

LATINO POLITICS IN CALIFORNIA

Edited by

Aníbal Yáñez-Chávez

CENTER FOR U.S.–MEXICAN STUDIES
UNIVERSITY OF CALIFORNIA, SAN DIEGO

Printed in the United States of America

Cover design by Siri Johansson, Sirious Design. "Su voto es su voz" art reproduced by permission of the Southwest Voter Registration Education Project.

ISBN 1-878367-34-X (pbk.)

Contents

Tables

Preface and Acknowledgments

The essays in this volume were originally prepared for a conference on "Latino Politics: An Analysis of Hispanic Political Participation in San Diego County," held at the Center for U.S.–Mexican Studies on May 3, 1996. The "Latino Politics" conference is a key example of the Center's strong commitment to public education. In particular, this project represents the Center's dedication to using its analytic resources and national research network to improve public understanding of issues directly relevant to the San Diego–Tijuana community. The Center is pleased to offer a public, nonpartisan forum for the discussion of contemporary issues such as Hispanic political participation in San Diego.

The vital question around which the conference was organized is the role that Latino voters and political activists are playing in reshaping the local and national political landscape. Although conference papers and discussions focused especially on developments in the San Diego area, participants examined such significant topics as the lessons to be learned from Latino and Latina political experiences in other parts of the United States, the main issues affecting Latinos in Southern California, who in the San Diego area's Latino community participates in politics and the reasons that most strongly motivate political involvement, and the strategies that offer the greatest potential for promoting Latino political participation in San Diego County.

The "Latino Politics" conference was the first activity undertaken in conjunction with the Center's recently established binational Community Advisory Board, whose eighteen distinguished members are listed at the back of this book. The Center established the Board in order to institutionalize its relations with the San Diego–Tijuana community and to identify potential research and public education projects of significant interest to the general public. On behalf of the Center for U.S.–Mexican Studies, I would like to thank all the Board's members for their invaluable support for this project.

Revised conference papers by Rodolfo O. de la Garza, Leo F. Estrada, Patricia Gándara, David G. Gutiérrez, and Carole J. Uhlaner appear in this volume. Víctor Calderón, Leo R. Chávez, Denise Moreno Ducheny, Stephen Erie, Paul Espinosa, Linda LeGerette, Art Madrid, Leonel Maldonado, Eliseo Medina, Michael R. Pfau, Art Torres, and David Valladolid greatly enriched debates at the conference in their role as panel discussants. In addition, Paule Cruz Takash, Andrés Jiménez, and Aníbal Yáñez-Chávez made important contributions as panel moderators. I also wish to thank Dr. Marjorie Caserio, Chancellor of the University of California, San Diego during 1995–1996, for her gracious welcome of conference participants. Aníbal Yáñez-Chávez generously agreed to take responsibility for editing conference papers for publication.

Many Center staff members and research affiliates were involved in the organization of the "Latino Politics" conference. C. R. Hibbs and Graciela Platero, program officers at the Center, demonstrated strong leadership in planning the conference program, fund raising, and establishing a highly visible profile for the conference in the San Diego–Tijuana community. Gabriela Lemus, a Guest Scholar at the Center during 1994–1996, ably served as conference rapporteur. Diana Platero, the Center's administrative specialist, did an outstanding job of coordinating logistics for the conference. In addition, the Center's undergraduate program assistants (Virginia Barreiro, Lily García, Adrián Hernández, Blanca Meléndrez, Lisette Robledo, Gabriela Sandoval, Lilia Soto, and Eduardo Zaldívar) all made a special effort to prepare for the conference.

The Center for U.S.–Mexican Studies gratefully acknowledges generous financial and in-kind contributions from the William and Flora Hewlett Foundation; the California Council for the Humanities; Oscar Padilla Mexican Insurance; the Center for the Study of Race and Ethnicity at the University of California, San Diego; the University of California Consortium on Mexico and the United States (UC MEXUS); the accounting firm of Calderon, Jaham, and Osborn; Radio Latina; and the Consulado General de México in San Diego.

KEVIN J. MIDDLEBROOK
DIRECTOR

1

Introduction: The Beat Goes On

Aníbal Yáñez-Chávez

The steady beat underlying this volume is demographics—the stormy, buffeted, but constant growth (both in absolute and in relative terms) of the Latino population (U.S.–born and immigrant) within the territorial boundaries of the United States. Just north of Latin America, on the California side of the U.S.–Mexico border, this beat may produce fear and loathing of "the other," or it may inspire hopes for a better day free of racism, discrimination, and poverty. Certainly the analytical use of the singular category Latino or Latina to include both U.S.–born "natives" of Mexican and Latin American descent and immigrants from all countries of Latin America (also blurring the racial and national diversity) is problematic, as are the categories Mexican American, Hispanic, or Chicano.

But whatever this population's divisions and its members' political or legal status, the increasing Latin American presence (and, in California, especially the Mexican and Central American presence) in the arts, science, politics, economics—indeed, all of society—is undeniable. Of course, the steady underlying beat of demographics is syncopated with the pounding of economic and political change inside the United States and Mexico. Thus, to a large extent the dynamics of

---

I would like to acknowledge the original drive and energy of C.R. Hibbs and Graciela Platero, who made this project a reality and were kind enough to invite my input in the early stages, as well as the persistence and patience of Kevin Middlebrook and Sandra del Castillo, without whose support the book would not have been brought to completion.

population geography in North America underlie the history, the key issues (immigration, education), and the changing politics of identity, class, and race that are raised in the contributions to this book.

The analysis of ethnic, and especially Latino, politics in the United States by the various contributors proceeds from the national framework to the reality of California. The following three chapters present a broad picture of the history, demography, and contemporary challenges of Latino ethnic politics in the United States. Rodolfo de la Garza unravels *"el cuento de los números"* (the notion that an increase in population automatically augments an ethnic group's political or electoral strength) and other Latino political myths. His explanation of how the political influence of population size is mediated by other factors lays the basis for Carole Uhlaner's detailed analysis of the participation and preferences of Latinos. But again, according to de la Garza, it is key to separate Mexican and Latino issues in order to understand them—and in order to understand the different ethnic politics of California, Texas, Miami, or New York.

In California, Mexican immigrants share traits that have regional political consequences. By definition, while they may be legal residents, they are not U.S. citizens, and five years after arrival is the soonest they are eligible to naturalize and then able to vote. More likely, they will never vote, as Mexicans historically have had some of the lowest U.S. naturalization rates among immigrants from all countries. It is also said that they tend to live in or create urban environments that are of little interest to most candidates for political office, a milieu that for its sights, sounds, and smells, its housing conditions, its language(s), its whatever, is not appealing to candidates. This, of course, may say less about Latinos than about those who choose to run for office, or the program and financing of the two-party system.

Uhlaner examines Latino politics from the perspective of ordinary participants, providing statistical parameters for thinking about ethnic politics in California. Not surprisingly, she finds that Latinos' demographic characteristics go along with lower participation in (electoral) politics: people with less money and less education are less active in politics (or, more precisely, are less apt to vote). And clearly those who do not have legal citizenship papers are specifically excluded from direct participation in the U.S. political system, as either candidates or voters.[1]

Taking up a number of these threads, Leo Estrada analyzes the demographic limitations to Latino political potential in California, from the shape of voting districts to the shape of the age pyramid, from class status to legal status. Estrada notes the geographic disper-

---

[1] There are some local exceptions to this rule, where noncitizen legal residents may run for office and vote in local school boards elections, for example.

sion of Latinos in San Diego, which is perhaps even greater than that of Latinos in most cities of the Southwest, where they also tend to be less residentially segregated than other groups. Even though it is a high-growth area for Latinos, San Diego County's urban sprawl accentuates that population's geographic dispersion (or fragmentation), and this may be less conducive to concerted political participation in elections. Paradoxically, the Latino population's characteristic that arguably gives it the greatest strength and hope for the future (its great youthfulness) is at the same time a major limitation to Latinos' electoral political participation. Noncitizenship and their disadvantaged position in a range of demographic factors associated with voting also limit Latinos' role in the electoral process. Despite these limitations, Latinos have been elected to local offices in San Diego; Estrada attributes this to Latino candidates' ability to win the support of non-Latino voters.

The last two chapters of this volume address two key issues that form the basis for much of Latino political involvement in California and shape it in determining ways: education and immigration. Patricia Gándara's contribution makes clear that the educational achievement of Latinos from kindergarten through high school and on into higher education remains a major challenge toward the end of the twentieth century, with significant political ramifications in terms of its potential to enhance or (in its absence) to deny Latino influence and power. Gándara reviews the national context of education for Latinos and a series of differing, although not necessarily incompatible, social science explanations of Latino educational failure. Proceeding to the California context, she analyzes a number of policy interventions aimed at changing the situation, from bilingual education through desegregation, including specific affirmative action programs (many of them under fire in the volatile political atmosphere of the 1990s).

Complementing recent studies that point to positive associations between school performance and the affirmation of collective ethnic identity among immigrant children (Rumbaut 1996; Rumbaut and Cornelius 1995), Gándara poses the implications of persistent educational failure and the changed political climate for social and education policy. Among her specific recommendations for California are that schools must nurture literacy in Latino students and families, that schools should not give up on desegregation, that society must find ways to put resources into programs to address the complex problem of high Latino dropout rates and thus avoid higher economic (and political) costs in the future, and that more universities should involve faculty in mentoring programs to help Latino and other minority students dream of a graduate education.

Last but not least, David Gutiérrez situates himself on the California–Mexico border to reflect upon migration and ethnic politics in an age which, as a result of dramatic global and regional shifts, has become transnational. But politics in California (electoral politics, at any rate) continues to be constrained not least of all by citizenship status and international boundaries. Gutiérrez finds that the current construction of the "immigration problem" is a simplistic and outmoded way of thinking about this human phenomenon, given the dramatic global and regional shifts in political economy. He argues that much of the public debate on immigration is ill grounded in a massive denial of the key role of Mexican immigrant workers in the southwestern United States over the last century. This limits the ability to understand the "immigration problem" as part of a long-standing geo-economic process. Today people no longer fit into the current U.S. system of bounded bipolar categories for human beings (native/foreigner, migrant/settler, citizen/alien), as circular migration and social networks between the United States and Mexico create different kinds of "communities": transnational networks (or circuits) whose existence is defined by people's movement across various North American regional spaces, not membership in one *or* another territorially defined community.

A recognition of regional interdependence between California and Mexico and an acknowledgment of the Latino presence in the Southwest are not enough. As traditional notions of community, polity, and nation undergo conflictive changes throughout the Americas, there is an urgent need to reframe the immigration debate, to view immigration (and by extension, ethnic politics as well) in the context of a broader regional system that includes, for example, the multifaceted role of the United States in drawing migrant labor out of Mexico. A Berlin Wall at the border will not change the reality that large numbers of non–U.S. citizens, including a relatively increasing number of Mexicans and Latinos, will continue to play a major role in the political economy of California and the region north of the border as a whole into the twenty-first century. This poses a number of key questions of human, civil, and political rights: Who deserves to be thought of as a member of our society? In the shadow of the specter of segmented citizenship, what is "our" society? The all-too-real danger is that the concept of membership in a transnational community or transnational process becomes a legal and political justification for denying immigrants rights and benefits where they live, work, and raise their children.

Two lines of thought emerge in this discussion, one that views political participation almost by definition as electoral politics, and another that views political participation as civic involvement in consciously shaping a community's or a region's life. If politics and political participation are only the electoral process (and the U.S. two-party system), demographics (one-third of all Latinos in San Diego are too young to vote) and citizenship or (un)documented status can lead to despair and to wallowing in marginality among Mexican immigrants themselves. Moreover, it can also push this "marginal" population to the margins of our own concerns. The confluence of politics and civil society in transnational spaces, on the other hand, may be generating novel forms of political participation, whether on the Internet, on a peace caravan to Chiapas, or in a union organizing drive.

Again, who or what is "our community"? Is there is a lag in awareness (or a denial) of a new social reality in California? What is the significance of the fact that while constituencies and constituents may be made up de facto of a limited subset of communities or societies, there are those who can unthinkingly refer to economic, social, and political hierarchies as ranked "scales of humanity" (see González et al. 1995)? Are demographic shifts indeed responsible for increasing racism, or does it have other roots?

These questions remain unanswered. But, as de la Garza points out, there is no doubt that Latino political reality is now part of the national agenda in the United States, whoever one may think speaks for Latinos (whether it is Latino academics, policy analysts, policy advocates—or youth demonstrating in the streets). And Latino politics is on the agenda even though at one level of analysis it may appear that ethnic mobilization per se has had limited political results. De la Garza points to the fact that Latinos mobilized to vote against the anti-immigrant and anti-Mexican Proposition 187 in California, and lost at the ballot box. This prominence of Latino issues and apparent failure of Latino mobilization around a crucial concern sharply poses the need for a long-term strategy of issued-based, cross-ethnic coalition building; for some, the most essential coalition for Latinos is with African Americans. For de la Garza, to chart a political course based on Latino ethnicity alone may perhaps produce fleeting good feelings, but it will surely lead to a continuous series of political defeats. (It should be noted, however, that there is no discussion here of independent political action, that is, independent of the two-party system.)

A key question is, indeed, who speaks for Latinos. Without a political party of their own, it makes a difference for analytical as much as for policy purposes when voice is extended to include not only academics, analysts, or advocates, but nameless daily border crossers (legal or not) and city youths. Whether the self-recognition and self-confidence gained by young Chicano students, for example, particularly in the exuberantly militant high school and community college walkouts against Proposition 187 in California, can be viewed as having no political results because the initiative passed at the polls is debatable. Within the U.S.–Mexico border region—and even in a wider North American political context—those youth mobilizations have had tremendous political impact and unleashed currents of energy and determination.

Given this panorama, what could be viable, successful strategies for encouraging Latino participation in politics? A number of California Latino politicians and community activists had experiences to share with the authors of these chapters at the conference that gave rise to the present volume (see below), pointing in general terms to an agenda for local action. Common needs such as jobs, greater educational opportunity, medical services, welfare, and public safety were identified as potential political demands. Diverse strategies to achieve them were presented, focusing on education, citizenship drives, lobbying, full utilization of community institutions, and organizing workers.

The discussion raised many questions, and partially answered a number of them. It was generally clear that measures like Proposition 187 are producing social, economic, and racial polarization, and by necessity result in many forms of political participation in response. There is broad agreement that coalitions are positive and necessary features of effective political participation; Latinos would have to outnumber Anglos by about three to one to determine their own future electorally. But coalitions with whom?—and around what concerns? Might active, issue-oriented coalitions be built across ethnic lines—for example, with African Americans to defend affirmative action, or with Southeast Asians to defend the rights of immigrants, or with the Anglo working class on economic issues, or with conservative Republicans (or, for that matter, Democrats) on "family values"? How do political-mobilization appeals to ethnicity intersect with the objective need for long-term issued-based alliances across ethnic lines, particularly for class solidarity?

For those who accept the claim that "San Diego is Republican," for example, and that politics is done only counting those who vote, then a strategy for coalition building in San Diego may mean alliances with GOP representations of "middle-class" interests. Other pragmatic, issue-based alliances might be sought based on resource complementarity (for example, "they have money, we have votes"), perhaps between Asians and Latinos. If one views the clarity and substance of a political program as key, one can ask whether the two-party system is a structural constraint to political participation to the extent that it does not address (or runs counter to) the needs and interests of vast swaths of the Latino population in economic distress. Indeed, in the midst of San Diego there are signs (among service industry workers and others) of the potential organizational power of a labor movement in which ethnicity and class intersect in positive, transforming directions, empowering and giving voice to ordinary working women and men.

It is true that actual guidelines for social organizing and coalition building are not the focus of the contributions to this volume, which reflect a certain tendency to look at politics in a more conventional or limited sense. Elections, after all, are the formal expression in a democracy of key social and economic relationships. Still, a practical understanding of political participation cannot be reduced or limited to elections and electoral activity every so many years; instead, there is a need to broaden the term to include the daily organizing efforts of unions on the job and of social movements in the community. The voice of young people, for example, is in the streets but not in this volume. The youth leaders in the MEChA (Movimiento Estudiantil Chicano de Aztlán) chapters throughout San Diego County who led high school walkouts and demonstrations against Proposition 187, the *Marchistas* who walked from Sacramento to San Diego in time for the Republican National Convention to protest Proposition 209 (the Orwellian "California Civil Rights Initiative")—their vision of politics and political participation is beyond the scope of this book.

Nevertheless, in a political season of third parties and maverick candidates, it is perhaps surprising that movement toward, or at least some discussion of, a nationalist party along the lines of La Raza Unida Party of Crystal City, Texas, is not a feature of the contributions to these pages. One might surmise that the politics of Chicano liberation (Rodríguez 1996) have been either forgotten or deemed anachronistic by the academic community. Whether or not this is true remains to be seen, as the structural characteristics and structural barriers affecting voter or citizenship participation become more apparent.

Because politics is more than elections, political mobilization may mean more than (or something other than) voter turnout. Perhaps scholars of Latino politics may discover more complex and powerful answers to the question, "why and how do Latinos participate politically?" through case studies or comparative ethnographic research on past experiences of political mobilization—the Alianza Federal de Mercedes (Federal Alliance of Land Grants) in Rio Arriba County, New Mexico; the Crusade for Justice in Colorado; La Raza Unida Party in Crystal City, Texas; and the struggle for community control of New York public schools, for example.[2] There is also still a need for studies that take a closer look at Latina women's political participation (along the lines of Ruiz 1987; Rose 1988; Santoli Pardo 1990; and

---

[2] That research remains to be done, but see M. García 1994; Busto 1991; I. García 1989; Santamaría 1989. For a recent documentary film treatment of some of these experiences, see Moreno and Galán 1996; Cozens 1996.

Apodaca 1994), which may result in a fuller understanding of the role of gender in ethnic politics.

Another important missing element for a book that had its origin in the San Diego area is an assessment, analysis, or discussion of the links between Latinos in San Diego County and politics in Mexico, the Tijuana region in particular (see Herzog 1990), or, more broadly, the "politics between Mexico and Aztlán" (Santamaría 1994). There is no discussion in these pages of San Diego's specificity as a city with large numbers of daily border crossers, most of them Mexicans. We still do not know much about the impact that Tijuana's contiguity has upon Latino politics in San Diego. Nor do we know whether the "democratization" politics of the PAN (National Action Party) in Baja California has regional repercussions to the north. Finally, we still know far too little about how increased immigration by indigenous people from southeastern Mexico to Baja California and California reshapes the ethnic politics of the North American immigrant stream (see Zabin 1992).

But the chapters of this book are a start. Originating as papers presented at a May 1996 conference organized by the Center for U.S.–Mexican Studies at the University of California, San Diego, on "Latino Politics: An Analysis of Hispanic Political Participation in San Diego County," they represent an honest attempt to link the academic work of scholars on Latino issues (immigration, education, demographics, history, political science analysis) with long-standing as well as new and urgent real-world problems and challenges facing Latinos and others. The conference brought together academic experts on Latinos' local and national political participation and Latino members of the San Diego region engaged in the practical experience of electoral politics, grassroots organizing, and community development. It sought and accomplished thoughtful interaction among academics, community representatives, and policy makers. It is hoped that the publication of this volume will further stimulate fruitful exchanges between the Center for U.S.–Mexican Studies and Chicanos, Hispanics, Latinos, Mexican Americans, and Mexicanos, and also serve to improve public understanding of issues directly relevant to the San Diego–Tijuana community.

References

Apodaca, María Linda. 1994. "They Kept the Home Fires Burning: Mexican-American Women and Social Change." Ph.D. thesis, University of California, Irvine.

Busto, Rudy Val. 1991. "Like a Mighty Rushing Wind: The Religious Impulse in the Life and Writing of Reies López Tijerina." Ph.D. thesis, University of California, Berkeley.

Cozens, Robert (producer). 1996. "Fighting for Political Power." Part 4 of 4-part mini-series *Chicano! History of the Mexican American Civil Rights Movement*. Documentary. PBS.

García, Ignacio M. 1989. *United We Win: The Rise and Fall of La Raza Unida Party*. Tucson: MASRC, University of Arizona.

García, Mario T. 1994. *Memories of Chicano History: The Life and Narrative of Bert Corona*. Berkeley: University of California Press.

González, Gerardo M., Francisco A. Ríos, Lionel A. Maldonado, and Stella T. Clark. 1995. "What's in a Name? Conflict at a University for the Twenty-first Century." In *The Leaning Ivory Tower: Latino Professors in American Universities*, edited by Raymond V. Padilla and Rudolfo Chávez Chávez. Albany: State University of New York Press.

Herzog, Lawrence A. 1990. *Where North Meets South: Cities, Space and Politics on the U.S.–Mexico Border*. Austin: Center for Mexican American Studies, University of Texas at Austin.

Moreno, Mylene, and Héctor Galán (producers). 1996. "Quest for a Home-land." Part 1 of 4-part mini-series *Chicano! History of the Mexican American Civil Rights Movement*. Documentary. PBS.

Rodríguez, Olga, ed. 1996. *The Politics of Chicano Liberation*. 2d ed. New York: Pathfinder.

Rose, Margaret Eleanor. 1988. "Women in the United Farm Workers: A Study of Chicana and Mexicana Participation in a Labor Union, 1950–1980." Ph.D. thesis, University of California, Los Angeles.

Ruiz, Vicki. 1987. *Cannery Women, Cannery Lives: Mexican Women, Unionization, and the California Food Processing Industry, 1930–1950*. Albuquerque: University of New Mexico Press.

Rumbaut, Rubén G. 1996. "The New Californians: Assessing the Educational Progress of Children of Immigrants," *CPS Brief* (California Policy Seminar, Berkeley) 8 (3).

Rumbaut, Rubén G., and Wayne A. Cornelius, eds. 1995. *California's Immigrant Children: Theory, Research, and Implications for Educational Policy*. U.S.–Mexico Contemporary Perspectives Series, no. 8. La Jolla: Center for U.S.–Mexican Studies, University of California, San Diego.

Santamaría, Arturo. 1989. "La izquierda norteamericana y los trabajadores indocumentados." In *Frontera norte: chicanos, pachucos y cholos*, edited by Luis Hernández Palacios and Juan Manuel Sandoval. México, D.F.: Universidad Autónoma de Zacatecas/Universidad Autónoma Metropolitana.

————. 1994. *La política entre México y Aztlán. Relaciones chicano mexicanas del 68 a Chiapas 1994*. Culiacán: Universidad Autónoma de Sinaloa/California State University, Los Angeles.

Santoli Pardo, Mary. 1990. "Identity and Resistance: Mexican-American Women and Grassroots Activism in Two Los Angeles Communities." Ph.D. thesis, University of California, Los Angeles.

Zabin, Carol. 1992. *Migración oaxaqueña a los campos agrícolas de California*. Current Issue Brief Series, no. 2. La Jolla: Center for U.S.–Mexican Studies, University of California, San Diego.

2

El Cuento de los Números and Other Latino Political Myths

Rodolfo O. de la Garza

Beginning in the 1970s, two myths were advanced to explain Latino political fortunes. The first, *"el cuento de los números,"* is a rhetorical message reminiscent of the story acted out in *"moros y cristianos,"* the Mexican colonial dance that symbolically reenacts the Christian defeat of the Moors in Spain. In its American manifestation, Latinos proclaim their imminent political defeat of Anglos, using census figures that show dramatic increases in the Hispanic population. The second, *"el desfile de la despreciada,"* brings to mind *"los machetes,"* a dance in which a woman flirts with three suitors, provoking them to fight for her favors. The contemporary version of this tale has become part of every presidential election since the mid-1970s: Hispanics, angry at having been taken advantage of in the past, wrap themselves in the assertion that they have become a decisive swing vote which will determine the election. They strut across the political stage, inviting presidential aspirants and political parties to prove themselves worthy of Latino affections.

Myths do not accurately reflect reality, however. More significantly, to the extent that they become ritualized, they may actually dampen the behavior they would promote. Americans, for example, have historically worshipped the principles of free speech and equality among citizens even as they have silenced those who challenge dominant mores and political beliefs and have discriminated against women and ethnic and racial groups. When criticized for this behavior, they often defend themselves by pointing to their myths. Myths, and the rituals that enshrine them, may also impede clear thinking. As long as Americans uncritically proclaim the myth of equal opportunity, they will find it difficult even to acknowledge that discrimination exists, much less analyze and overcome it.

The *"cuento de los números,"* *"la despreciada,"* and other less rooted tales appear to be having the same impact on Latino political life that American celebrations of equality have on the nation's willingness to deal with inequality. That is, they have become so important that reality is ignored. Although myths are an essential part of life, and Latinos, like the nation, need them, there is an equal or greater need to examine the realities of Latino political life. That is the aim of this chapter: it examines the realities that political myths claim to portray in the hope that this will stimulate serious discussion regarding the future roles Latinos will play in our nation's politics.

Latino Demographics

Because it focuses only on population growth, *"el cuento de los números"* misrepresents how demographic changes are affecting Latino political fortunes. While increased numbers are central to Hispanic politics, the effects of changes in the composition of the population, its geographic dispersion, and basic characteristics such as age, education, and income must also be taken into account. These changes have both enhanced and diminished Latino political clout historically and may continue to do so in the future.

The growth, diversification, and dispersion of the Latino population are incontrovertible. The 1970 census counted 9.1 million Latinos in the nation, most of whom were U.S.–born Mexican Americans living in the Southwest. By 1990, Hispanics totaled 21.8 million, an increase of over 135 percent. Although over 60 percent were of Mexican origin, other groups were now substantially represented: 12 percent were Puerto Ricans, 6 percent came from Central America, 5 percent came from Cuba and from South America, respectively, and Dominicans accounted for 2 percent. Furthermore, and perhaps more importantly, the ratio of native born to immigrants decreased substantially and varied dramatically across subgroups. Overall, while the U.S. born made up 59 percent of all Latinos, they accounted for 67 percent of Mexicans, 28 percent of Cubans, 55 percent of Puerto Ricans, and 46 percent of all other Hispanics. Equally significant, the majority of Cubans and 49 percent of Puerto Ricans came to the United States before 1970, while 51 percent of Mexican and 58 percent of "other Hispanic" immigrants came after 1980 (TRC 1995a: 5–6). Also, by 1990 Latinos were dispersed across the nation and had become a national rather than a regional minority (see table 2.1).

These demographic transformations impact Latino politics in several ways. First, size and dispersion create the condition for Latinos to have a national voice. In the absence of either, Hispanic national influence would decrease substantially. Second, because of the 1965 Voting Rights Act (VRA) and its subsequent renewals and Supreme Court interpretations, population size has been the principal factor explaining electoral representation (de la Garza and DeSipio 1993). That is, for the past twenty years, and especially during the past decade, the VRA has required that electoral districts for entities ranging from the U.S. Congress to school boards include majority-minority districts (those in which minorities are the majority of a district's residents) in a number that reflects the size of the minority population within the geographic boundaries of the electoral entity. Thus, between 1984 and 1994, the number of Latino elected officials expanded by 48 percent, close to the 50 percent growth in population over the same period (NALEO 1994: xi). It should be noted that the increase in elected officials did not come automatically but was instead largely the result of successful litigation initiated by Latino politicos and supported by mobilized Latino communities, with the assistance of organizations such as the Mexican American Legal Defense and Education Fund (MALDEF) and the Southwest Voter Registration and Education Project (SVREP) armed with the VRA requirements.

Third, the diversification of the population has, to some extent, mitigated the political gains produced by population growth. This is most notable as a consequence of the increased proportion of immigrants who share two traits that negatively affect political participation, especially voting. First, if they are legal resident aliens, they are ineligible to vote in any election (from local to national level) in virtually every electoral district in the nation until they naturalize.[1] In most cases, this postpones voting for a period of at least five years. And immigrants who are undocumented and do not legalize their status will never be eligible to vote. Second, Hispanic immigrants have a low propensity to naturalize even after they are eligible to do so. This has been especially true of Mexican immigrants, who are the largest immigrant group in the nation and have the second lowest naturalization rates (INS 1993: 132). The impact on Hispanic political clout is indicated by the fact that in 1994 the number of Latinos ineligible to vote because they were not citizens exceeded the number of Latino voters (TRC 1995b: 3–7). Naturalization rates may increase because California's Proposition 187 and the anti-immigrant rhetoric of the 1996 presidential campaign have spurred great increases in naturalization applications. For reasons described below, however, this will not necessarily translate into a comparably large increase in the number of voters.

---

[1] A few school boards allow noncitizen resident aliens to vote.

TABLE 2.1
LATINO POPULATION IN TEN LARGEST STATES,
AND TEN STATES WITH THE HIGHEST PERCENTAGES OF LATINOS, 1990

State	Electoral Votes	Latino Population	Percent Latino	Largest Latino Group(s)	Percent Largest Group	Percent Foreign Born
California	52	7,687,938	25	Mexican	81	47
New York	31	2,221,402	12	Puerto Rican	49	54
Texas	30	4,339,905	25	Mexican	91	28
Florida	23	1,574,143	12	Cuban	43	68
Pennsylvania	21	232,262	2	Puerto Rican	66	42
Illinois	20	904,446	8	Mexican	69	48
Ohio	19	139,696	1	Mexican	37	30
				Puerto Rican	36	
Michigan	16	185,900	2	—	—	16
New Jersey	13	740,000	8	Puerto Rican	40	62
North Carolina	12	66,290	1	—	—	34
Massachusetts	10	288,000	4	Puerto Rican	54	58
Arizona	6	688,000	19	Mexican	91	25
Colorado	6	424,000	12	Mexican	96[1]	12
New Mexico	3	579,000	38	Mexican	100[1]	3

[1]Because of the distinctive history of these two states, these totals include respondents who identify as "Spanish" and "Other Hispanic."
Source: TRC 1995a.

The increased proportion of immigrants among the Latino population has not enhanced—and may have diminished—Latino political clout in statewide elections such as those for governor and senator. In California, for example, in 1988 and 1992 Latinos constituted 8 and 10 percent of the electorate, respectively, even though they were 25 percent of the state's population. Because immigrants live in working-class, ethnic-enclave neighborhoods, they contribute to creating an environment that political candidates for statewide offices find unattractive. That is, these neighborhoods include so many people who are unlikely to vote—noncitizens and citizens with low income and education levels—that candidates seldom campaign there (de la Garza, Menchaca, and DeSipio 1994). Citizens in these neighborhoods are largely ignored, and thus these major elections seldom result in a highly mobilized Latino vote.

Also, for reasons that are not yet completely understood, Latino immigrants who do naturalize vote at lower rates than comparably situated U.S.–born citizens (DeSipio 1996). This may well be explained by how immigrants are socialized into American politics: they hold jobs that are unlikely to be a source of political education, and they live in neighborhoods where there are few continuous signs of political life and that are seldom targeted for mobilization by political candidates. In other words, there are few opportunities for immigrants to learn positive lessons that would motivate them to be politically active. Consequently, they engage the polity at even lower rates than their U.S.–born counterparts. Ironically, then, increased naturalization rates could actually depress electoral participation even as the number of Latino voters rises.

Age, education, and income also affect political participation. Political activities such as voting increase with age. Latinos, however, are much younger than non-Hispanic whites. In 1994, the median age for Anglos was thirty-four, compared to twenty-five for Latinos; and 36 percent of Latinos were under eighteen years of age, compared to 26 percent of Anglos. Furthermore, because of immigration and high birth rates, Latinos are aging more slowly than Anglos. In 1983, the median age for Latinos was twenty-three, only one year less than in 1994. Citizens over sixty-five years of age have the highest voting rates. In 1990 this cohort made up 14 percent of the Anglo population but only 6 percent of Latinos. However, eighteen- to twenty-four-year-olds, the cohort with the lowest participatory rates, makes up 12 percent of Latinos compared to 10 percent of Anglos (TRC 1995b: 13–15).

Income and education affect political involvement similarly, and this also disadvantages Hispanics. In 1992, the median income for non-Hispanic white families was $40,420, while for Latinos (including citizens and noncitizens) it was $23,912. Almost 25 percent of all Latino families lived below the poverty line in 1990, compared to 7 percent of Anglo families. In 1994, 15 percent of Hispanics had eight years or less of schooling; 35 percent had at least some college. In contrast, almost half of all Anglos had at least some college, and only 6.6 percent had had eight years of school or less (TRC 1995b: 16–21).

Contrary to *"el cuento de los números,"* then, dramatically increased numbers do not automatically generate increased political influence. Instead, the political significance of population size is mediated by other factors. With regard to elections, Latino numbers have a direct and immediate impact in areas that are so overwhelmingly Hispanic that Hispanics invariably seek and win office. Latino population size had also, until 1995, been important in jurisdictions governed by the VRA, which have been required to maximize the number of majority-minority districts given the size of their Latino populations. These districts, it should be noted, are designed to increase the probability of electing a Hispanic, but they do not increase, and may dampen, Hispanic voter turnout (de la Garza and DeSipio 1993). Additionally, the constitutionality of these districts is now under review by the U.S. Supreme Court. Its decision, expected by the end of the 1996 term, will not enhance but could greatly diminish the impact of population size as a factor in Latino political fortunes.

The impact of the population boom is barely visible in statewide contests. Between 1984 and 1994, the number of Hispanic elected officials increased from 3,128 to 4,625, but the 1994 number included only eight officials elected to statewide offices. Six of these were in New Mexico, which has a long tradition of electing Hispanic officials. Moreover, while the dramatic increases in population surely account for some of the increased turnout between the 1988 and 1992 presidential elections (table 2.2), they did not have a similar uniform effect on midterm elections between 1990 and 1994 (table 2.3). More significantly, Latino turnout has not increased relative to Anglo turnout in recent elections. Thus, not only has increased population not enabled Latinos to elect their own to statewide positions, but this growth has not prevented a decline in Hispanics' ability to increase their influence in the election of governors, senators, and presidents in recent years (de la Garza and DeSipio 1996).

Another factor limiting the significance of increased numbers in national elections is that, to date, Hispanics are not a homogeneous political community. Depending on the issue, differences in national origin, nativity, and state of residence produce important schisms. For example, there is widespread agreement across national-origin groups regarding language policy and government spending on key domestic issues, but there are noteworthy differences regarding foreign policy. This has potentially divisive consequences, as was evident when all Mexican American congressmen but one voted in favor of the North American Free Trade Agreement (NAFTA), while all the

Puerto Rican and Cuban American representatives voted against it. The significance of nativity is evident with regard to immigration policy. Latino immigrants think that U.S. immigration policy should give preference to Latin Americans, and they do not feel that there are too many immigrants entering the country. U.S.–born Latinos hold exactly opposite positions on these two points (de la Garza et al. 1992).

TABLE 2.2
LATINO VOTE IN PRESIDENTIAL ELECTIONS, 1988–1992

State	1988 Vote (1000s)	1992 Vote (1000s)	% Change, 92–88	% of Total Vote, 1988	% of Total Vote, 1992	% Change, % 92– % 88
Arizona	119	156	31.1	8.9	9.0	0.1
California	827	1,135	37.2	7.9	9.6	1.7
Colorado	137	136	-1.0	8.9	8.0	-0.9
Florida	361	411	13.8	7.0	7.1	0.1
Illinois	154	171	11.0	3.0	3.0	0.0
New Jersey	141	173	22.7	4.1	4.8	0.7
New Mexico	161	172	6.8	28.4	25.5	-2.9
New York	411	382	-7.1	5.7	5.0	-0.7
Texas	854	927	8.5	13.8	13.6	-0.2

Where Hispanics live also affects their opinions in ways that further complicate the viability of a unified front. For example, Latinos in Florida and Texas have relatively similar views regarding immigration and police relations even though the Latino populations of these states comprise primarily Cuban Americans and Mexican Americans, respectively. Similarly, Puerto Ricans and other Hispanics in New York closely resemble Mexican Americans in California regarding these same issues (TRC 1996).

The population boom, then, is not the political panacea most Hispanic leaders predicted. Given the structure of the American polity, numbers are a potentially valuable resource, but their ultimate significance can only be understood in relation to other factors. Moreover, numbers may also be the source of political problems. This was evident in the debate over Proposition 187 and in the continuing efforts to make English the nation's official language. These examples suggest that unless Latinos convert their numbers into usable political currency (votes), their increased population may actually be a handicap rather than an advantage. Further, even if they do increase their political currency, they will have to invest it wisely or it will dissipate or be devalued. It is also possible that the continued repetition of the "numbers myth" may lull Hispanic voters into a sense of false confidence or generate alienation. Why should they mobilize if their numbers assure them victory? And how will they react if they participate, only to find that the power of their numbers was overstated?

TABLE 2.3
LATINO VOTE IN 1990 AND 1994 MIDTERM ELECTIONS

State	1990 Vote (1000s)	1994 Vote (1000s)	% Change, 94–90	% of Total Vote, 1990	% of Total Vote, 1994	% Change, % 94– % 90
Arizona	88	120	36.4	8.9	9.0	0.1
California	844	1,134	34.4	7.9	9.6	0.1
Colorado	64	45	-29.7	8.9	8.0	-0.9
Florida	301	263	-12.6	7.0	7.1	0.1
Illinois	114	117	2.6	3.0	3.0	0.0
New Jersey	96	82	-14.6	4.1	4.8	0.7
New Mexico	126	144	14.3	28.4	25.5	-2.9
New York	345	291	-15.7	5.7	5.0	-0.7
Texas	605	734	21.3	13.8	13.6	-0.2

Latino Partisanship and the Swing Vote

"El desfile de la despreciada" has as its foundation the claims of *"el cuento de los números."* However, it adds two components. The first concerns Latino partisanship. Citing Hispanic family values, support for economic individualism, and patriotism as evidence that Hispanics are Republican fellow travelers, the GOP is assiduously courting Latinos to convert them into full-fledged party members (de la Garza and DeSipio 1992, 1996). Democrats, on the other hand, take Latinos

for granted (Subervi-Vélez 1992; Morris 1992; Lubenow 1991). The heads of Latino organizations combine Republicans' claims with their resentment against the Democrats' nonresponsiveness to proclaim that the Latino vote is up for grabs. Arturo Vargas, executive director of the National Association of Latino Elected and Appointed Officials, for example, stated: "I think in the current environment, Latinos are very eager to be heard. I can easily see Latinos voting for Republicans who are supportive of people of immigrant backgrounds, like George Bush, Jr." (Torres 1995). This leads to the second part of the fable: spokesmen paint the picture of a unified electorate under their control which can be delivered to whichever party is most responsive to Hispanic needs. Because of the size of the Latino electorate (the "numbers" fable), they proclaim that this will guarantee victory to the deserving suitor.

There are several serious problems with this claim. First, while it is true that Latinos agree with Republicans regarding some issues, they disagree on many more. For example, a survey of Hispanics in California, Texas, Florida, and New York found that the majority of Latinos believe that people are on welfare because they do not want to work (TRC 1996: 12). And yet, Hispanic domestic spending priorities manifest strong support for New Deal/War on Poverty–type programs (de la Garza et al. 1992: 90–91). In the area of cultural policy, a cornerstone of Republican appeals, the majority of Mexican Americans, Puerto Ricans, and Cuban Americans disagree with the Republican position that advocates making English the nation's official language. Additionally, the great majority of all three groups supports bilingual education, believes that public services should be provided in Spanish, and disagrees that businesses have the right to require employees to speak English during working hours (de la Garza et al. 1992: 97–99). Furthermore, the survey found that:

- close to three-quarters of respondents support continuing affirmative action;

- between 44 percent (in Texas) and 68 percent (in New York) disagree that police in their local communities treat Anglos and Latinos equally; and

- majorities in each state—ranging from 56 percent in Texas to 79 percent in Florida—favor providing government services beyond emergency health care to undocumented immigrants (TRC 1996).

Clearly, Latino values and policy preferences do not indicate widespread endorsement of Republican policy objectives. Curiously, this applies even to Cuban Americans, who register overwhelmingly as Republicans. This may explain why on many domestic issues Cuban Americans and their legislators in Florida look more like Democrats than Republicans (Moreno and Warren 1992: 136–38).

Hispanic partisanship reflects these policy preferences; approximately 60 percent of Latinos who are members of a political party are Democrats. Furthermore, this has not changed much since 1980 (see table 2.4). Republican identification has increased, however, and this probably reflects the results of a few formerly independent voters becoming Republicans and of new voters who begin their partisan life in the Grand Old Party. The latter pattern is evident in the fact that among Mexican Americans between the ages of eighteen and twenty-four, strong Democrats outnumber strong Republicans by a ratio of two to one; among those aged thirty-five to fifty, this increases to over ten to one; and for those sixty-six years of age and older, the ratio is greater than thirty to one (García et al. n.d.). It is also important to note that Hispanics almost always vote for Democrats at rates that exceed their party identification in both presidential and congressional races (Brischetto 1995; de la Garza and DeSipio 1992: 8).

TABLE 2.4
HISPANIC PARTY IDENTIFICATION, 1980–1994
(PERCENTAGES)

Year	Republican	Independent	Democrat
1994	30	9	61
1992	25	21	55
1984	21	22	57
1980	23	15	62

Source: Brischetto 1995.

A final indicator of the extent of Latino partisanship is the ratio of Democratic to Republican Hispanic elected officials. In 1994, of 2,255 Latino elected officials who are members of a political party, only 8 percent were Republicans. Curiously, California had 25 percent of these, while Florida, which is thought to be the hotbed of Hispanic Republicanism, had only 17 percent (NALEO 1994: xi).

In sum, there is no evidence that Latinos are a "swing vote," available to whichever party offers the highest bid. Instead, Latinos are strong and loyal partisans—and divided in their loyalties. Cuban Americans are Republicans, while Mexican Americans and Puerto Ricans are Democrats. Furthermore, it is not necessarily true that Latinos lose influence because they are loyal partisans. To the contrary, in presidential elections and other statewide contests, their staunch partisanship provides them the opportunity to become increasingly important members of their respective parties. Several examples illustrate why this is so.

In the 1996 Texas Democratic senatorial primary, Víctor Morales, a teacher with virtually no political experience or capital, was the top vote getter; he eliminated one former congressman and forced a second into a runoff. Morales won the nomination with 51.2 percent of the vote, even though his opponent had the endorsement of virtually every major state Democratic leader. Mr. Morales's victory met the major requirements for Latinos to influence statewide elections (Guerra 1992):

- they must unite behind one candidate;

- it must be a highly competitive election;

- the election must include other campaigns in which Latinos are major contestants (Latinos were contesting congressional seats in El Paso and South Texas, areas with high Latino concentrations); and

- the campaign must mobilize Hispanics without generating a counter-mobilization among non-Hispanics.

Morales's victory also illustrates how strong partisanship enhances Hispanic influence. Statewide turnout for the runoff election was 5 percent, but in Latino precincts it was 14 percent, making approximately half of the votes in the runoff election Latino votes. Morales won 67 percent of these Latino votes and a minority of non-Hispanic votes, securing him the Democratic Party's senatorial nomination (McNeely 1996).

Morales's triumph also suggests the costs of intense partisanship. His victory would have been impossible if Anglos had voted in greater numbers. The major reason for the low Anglo turnout appears to be that Anglo Democrats are becoming an endangered species in Texas. That is, Anglos have switched to the Republican Party in such numbers that their influence in the Democratic Party has greatly declined. This switch also means that Latinos would be hard pressed to be major players in the Republican Party even if they joined it in large numbers. Thus, Anglo voters voice their preferences in the Republican primary and the general election. Morales may have won a Pyrrhic victory: in a state where Latinos comprise less than 15 percent of the electorate and in which the Democratic Party is in the minority, not even a mobilized Latino electorate is likely to safeguard him from a resounding defeat in November.

In 1994, partisanship enabled Latinos to determine the outcome of the California senatorial election. Energized in opposition to Proposition 187, Latino voter turnout reached 1,134,000, from 844,000 voters in 1990, an increase of 34 percent. The 1994 campaign included three high-profile contests: the race for governor, pitting Pete Wilson against Kathleen Brown; the California Senate race, with Dianne Feinstein running against Michael Huffington; and Proposition 187. In effect, these merged into a single campaign that took on an intensely anti-immigrant, anti-Mexican tone. On one side were Michael Huffington, Pete Wilson, and Prop. 187 supporters. Dianne Feinstein, Kathleen Brown, and the great majority of Latinos were on the other. Feinstein's case is noteworthy because she did not make her views on Proposition 187 known until just before the election. Latinos voted three to one against Proposition 187 (TRC 1996: 23) and two to one for Ms. Feinstein.

Proposition 187 passed overwhelmingly, but Feinstein won a narrow victory. Anglo voters had so strongly endorsed Proposition 187 that Latino opposition was essentially meaningless. Anglos also favored Huffington over Feinstein by 48 to 44 percent. Feinstein's margin of victory was less than 200,000 votes, but her margin among Latinos was over 400,000 (Southwest Voter Registration Institute 1994). Feinstein won because Latinos voted cohesively and in high numbers in her favor, even though she never spoke out against Proposition 187 during the campaign. Why did Latinos support her? Because she ran as a Democrat. Why were Latinos able to influence the outcome of the election? Because the election met what may be the two most important conditions for Latino electoral influence: a highly competitive race and a highly mobilized and cohesive Hispanic electorate.

As in the Morales example, however, the long-term gains of this case are unclear. Senator Feinstein has never acknowledged her debt to the Latino community. Furthermore, she is increasingly advocating positions that are at odds with Hispanic preferences. Thus, even though Latinos were critical to her election, it appears that Feinstein feels free to ignore them in favor of increasing her support among Anglos. She may believe that the 1994 election was aberrant in how it divided Anglos and with regard to its high Latino turnout, or that Latinos will vote for her in her next campaign because, as was true in 1994, they will not be welcomed by Republican candidates. In this case, then, partisanship enabled Latino voters to make a difference, but Latino leaders have been unable to convert this into political capital for the community.

The third example of the benefits of partisanship is evident in presidential campaigns. In 1988, Mexican Americans were essential to Michael Dukakis's primary victory in Texas, which propelled him to the Democratic nomination (de la Garza and DeSipio 1992). Unfortunately, the significance of this contribution was lost in President Bush's resounding victory. In 1992 the closeness of the Bush–Clinton–Perot race provided Latinos an opportunity to influence the outcome in six of the nine states in which Latinos were a significant portion of the electorate. That potential influence was predicated on high partisanship rather than on switching parties. In Colorado, New Jersey, and New Mexico, for example, Latino Democratic support usually varies from 65 to 75 percent in two-person elections. Because Perot's candidacy had altered traditional voting patterns among the Anglo electorate, Clinton only needed 49, 46, and 28 percent, respectively, of the Latino vote to carry these intensely contested states. It would have been extremely difficult for Latinos to have become a meaningful swing vote in these states—that is, to have voted Republican in numbers sufficient to produce a Democratic defeat. Instead, Latinos remained loyal to the Democrats and contributed to, and in Colorado may have accounted for, Clinton's victory. In Florida, where the election was also highly competitive, the same pattern exists in reverse. Florida Republicans count on 70 percent support from Cuban Americans. However, to win in 1992 they only needed 25 percent of the Hispanic vote. Again, it would have a required a "swing" of unprecedented proportions to have Cubans vote Democratic in numbers sufficient to enable them to influence the outcome of the election (de la Garza and DeSipio 1996: 30–34). Cubans remained faithful Republicans and helped Bush carry the state.

Clearly the evidence does not support claims that Latinos are swing voters. Furthermore, to the extent that Republican affiliation is increasing among younger Hispanics, the new pattern portends realignment, not swinging. In the current political climate, it is also unclear why political leaders think that threats of abandoning the Democrats would be credible. Given their demographic characteristics and cultural commitments, it is hard to imagine that Latinos would find the Republican agenda appealing. Additionally, efforts by organizational leaders to move the electorate away from the Democrats would surely produce quick and devastating retaliation from virtually every Hispanic Democratic elected official in the nation.

Rather than play the courtesan, organizational leaders would be better served if they found ways to mobilize the large proportion of Hispanic citizens who are unconnected to the political process. If these citizens could be energized, their partisanship would force the Democratic Party to be more attentive and inclusive. Additionally, an energized Latino electorate could also awaken genuine interest among Republicans which could, in turn, lead to moderating the

GOP's platform. If that occurred, Latinos might listen to Republican appeals, and a Hispanic swing vote could become a real possibility.

Who Speaks for Latinos?

To some, the answer to this question is, "we do, because los pobrecitos no entienden," a response akin to "elitelore" (Wilkie 1973) which, given its content, is unlikely to be popularized. Essentially it means that because Hispanic realities are too complex to be measured by surveys in the ways that all other segments of society are, or because Latinos are too ignorant to respond to such surveys or understand their own interests, Latino preferences and realities can be accurately depicted only by community "representatives." The three principal purveyors of this message are Latino academics who dismiss the results of quantitative social science research (including public opinion surveys), policy analysts supported by conservative organizations, and Hispanic community advocates.

The least influential members of this triad are the academics. Survey research consistently shows that on most issues, Hispanic social and political preferences and behaviors fall well within the mainstream of American society (de la Garza and Weaver 1985; Los Angeles Times 1983; de la Garza et al. 1992). However, this contradicts the picture that many academics paint. For example, many in the academy claim that Latinos stand together with African Americans and other ethnic/racial groups as "people of color" against whites (Anglos). However, most Hispanics in the United States identify as white (Bean and Tienda 1987: 38), and there is widespread evidence regarding the tenuousness of Hispanic–African American coalitions (Tedin and Murray 1994). Also, the results of the Latino National Political Survey (LNPS) confirm in detail what the census reports (see TRC 1995a)—that Hispanic immigrants rapidly acquire English and that U.S.–born Latinos report much higher English abilities than Spanish abilities (de la Garza et al. 1992: 42–43).

The LNPS was developed by four bilingual codirectors—with the assistance of an advisory board, which included two of the nation's most prominent Latino (bilingual) social scientists writing about the centrality of bilingualism to the Hispanic community, and a survey director who is recognized as the leading expert on bilingual surveys of the Hispanic population. Yet a group of academic critics tried to dismiss the LNPS findings because, they claimed, the survey was developed from a "monolingual perspective" (Fraga et al. 1994: 12). This posturing has less to do with epistemological biases than with political disagreements. That is, when research presents a picture that reinforces what academics proclaim, they embrace it; when it contradicts them, they challenge it on the grounds that their understanding supersedes such findings.

More significant for Hispanic political well-being is how Hispanic advocates and conservative policy "analysts" challenge each other's claims regarding what Hispanics think and who represents them. On the one hand, both recognize the validity of survey and other empirical research methods; on the other, each accepts only those data that support their claims, and they disregard or distort all other results. For example, Linda Chávez, a leading conservative policy spokesperson, testified before the House Judiciary Committee in April 1996 against bilingual ballots on the grounds that "bilingual ballots have had no effect on Hispanic voter turnout, because in fact they should almost never be necessary. In order to vote, one must be a citizen, and in order to become a citizen one must be proficient in English." Chávez buttresses her argument with reference to a Tomás Rivera Center report that found that low education and high noncitizenship rates were the principal factors explaining low rates of Hispanic voter participation. However, the TRC report never mentioned bilingual ballots, and Chávez provided no evidence regarding the language characteristic of Latino citizens or how widely bilingual ballots are used. Given that she is a native of New Mexico, a state where many older Hispanics are Spanish dominant, Ms. Chávez must know that many U.S.–born Latinos know little English. And, as table 2.5 illustrates, Spanish-dominant U.S.–born Hispanics and naturalized citizens are found across the nation.

Thus, not only does Ms. Chávez ignore the extent of Spanish dominance among the U.S. born, but she also greatly overstates the English abilities of naturalized citizens. This is most evident among Cuban American citizens, the great majority of whom are naturalized. Perhaps even more significant is that most of those who say their Spanish is superior to their English report low English literacy (de la Garza et al. 1992: 66). Furthermore, when Spanish-dominant Latino voters know that Spanish-language ballots are available, they use them and find them helpful (see table 2.6). Clearly, then, such citizens would be effectively disenfranchised if Spanish-language ballots were discontinued. Ms. Chávez is familiar with the language abilities of Hispanics and should be familiar with all of the data included here. Her failure to incorporate this information into her argument would seem to have less to do with objectively determining the need for language services among Hispanic voters than with her continuing effort to have her views, rather than those of other Latino leaders, define Latino political realities (Chávez 1991).

Peter Skerry, another conservative analyst, also uses distorted data to claim that Mexican American leaders are misrepresenting their constituents. For example, a 1981–82 survey found that 93 and 82 percent of Mexican Americans in San Antonio and Los Angeles, respectively, favored bilingual education (de la Garza and Brischetto 1983: 9); in 1990 the LNPS found that the overwhelming majority of Mexican Americans, Puerto Ricans, and Cubans across the nation shared this view (de la Garza et al. 1992: 99). Skerry nonetheless asserts that "a discernible segment of Mexican Americans is hostile to [bilingual education]" (Skerry 1993). Like Chávez, Skerry had accurate data regarding Mexican American views on this issue. That he willfully distorted these views suggests how little respect he has for Mexican American public opinion and the intensity of his efforts to be the official interpreter of Mexican American realities.

TABLE 2.5
ENGLISH-LANGUAGE ABILITIES OF HISPANIC CITIZENS

Group	Percent U.S.–born, 18–64 Years, Who Don't Speak English Well or Speak No English	Percent U.S.–born, 65+ Years, Who Don't Speak English Well or Speak No English	Percent U.S.–born & Naturalized, 18 Years +, Spanish Monolinguals or Better in Spanish
Puerto Ricans in New York	24	68	—
Mexican Americans in Los Angeles	8	13	—
Mexican Americans in Chicago	8	13	—
Mexican Americans in Houston	7	21	—
Mexican Americans Nationwide	—	—	12
Puerto Ricans Nationwide	—	—	41
Cuban Americans Nationwide	—	—	43

Sources: 1990 U.S. census, 5 percent PUMS, de la Garza et al. 1992: 65.

TABLE 2.6
SPANISH-BALLOT AVAILABILITY AND UTILIZATION BY
SPANISH-DOMINANT HISPANIC VOTERS
(PERCENTAGES)

	Mexican Americans	Puerto Ricans	Cuban Americans
Spanish Ballots Were Available	69	48	74
Used Spanish Ballots or Spanish and English Ballots	62	73	77
Spanish Ballots Were Helpful	49	36	48

Source: de la Garza et al. 1992.

Some Hispanic community advocates sometimes behave similarly. For example, in 1994 the Southwest Voter Research Institute found that 55 percent of Texas Mexican Americans and 40 percent of those in California supported a national ID card (Southwest Voter Research Institute 1994); the Tomás Rivera Center found almost identical results in 1995 (TRC 1996). Some Hispanic advocates and a few legislators angrily dismissed these findings. Illustrative of their criticisms are the comments by a representative of the National Council of La Raza (NCLR): "The questions were insufficient and failed to take into account the full impact of current legislation that has a detrimental effect on the community" (Torres 1996: 4). NCLR's president went on to warn against "undue media attention to surveys which purport to represent the 'true' sentiment of the Latino community." He was especially critical because these polls placed "Latino sentiment on immigration at odds with 'every Latino organization and every Hispanic member of Congress on both sides of the aisle'" (Tilove 1996). Taken together, these views suggest that some community advocates believe Hispanics are not competent to know their own interests, and that policy makers should pay more attention to community advocates than to the community itself. That interpretation is consistent with the NCLR president's support of the nation's new border enforcement policies which include building walls and fences along the U.S.–

Mexico border (Pear 1996: 8) despite widespread opposition to these efforts from Latinos across the country (TRC 1996: 10).

That there are differences between leaders and the average citizen regarding any particular policy is to be expected. However, it is fundamentally undemocratic, in the face of such differences, for leaders of community organizations to dismiss the views of those they claim to represent. Indeed, it is precisely such behavior that critics such as Chávez and Skerry cite as evidence that Hispanic leaders do not represent their constituencies.

Their limitations notwithstanding, public opinion polls are essential to American politics. Until recently, however, pollsters seldom reported Hispanic perspectives (de la Garza 1987). Because of the growth in the Hispanic population and its increased political influence, this is now changing; and along with other Americans, Latinos are being asked their opinions regarding all of the issues that make up the nation's political agenda. Some of these polls are publicly reported; others are conducted privately by candidates and parties. Whether or not Latino advocates know about or acknowledge the results of these polls, they may be certain that policy makers and political leaders will use them. The Latino community must therefore learn to use this information to hold accountable anyone, Latino and Anglo alike, who would speak in their name or who deals with issues that concern them. To do otherwise is to court paternalism and unresponsive leadership. If Latino advocates, academics, and others who claim to speak for Hispanics are dissatisfied with what their "constituents" have to say, they should either convince them to change their minds or, that having failed, desist from claiming to speak on behalf of the community.

Conclusion

Population growth has transformed Latino political realities. Whether or not they are citizens who register and vote, Latinos have altered the nation's politics. This is why Republicans intermittently woo them and why Democrats are sometimes very attentive to them. This also explains why national pollsters, especially those in key states with large Hispanic populations such as Texas and California, have begun systematically to measure Latino public opinion.

Numbers alone do not count for much, however. Their impact is enhanced or diminished by factors such as the group's distinctiveness and coherence, the ways and extent to which it engages the polity, and institutional arrangements and practices within mainstream society that facilitate or impede political engagement.

At present these factors are working at cross-purposes. Numbers and some institutional rules such as the Voting Rights Act are increasing the number of Latino elected officials at local levels, but their impact diminishes at higher rungs on the ladder of political offices. Moreover, the same rules that increase representation may decrease voting—which, in turn, diminishes Hispanic influence in the most important elections.

Similarly, party loyalty has enabled Hispanics to become a significant force in the Democratic Party, especially in the Southwest. However, if current trends continue and Republicans build on their 1994 congressional takeover, this may become akin to being first mate on the Titanic.

Increased numbers also affect ethnic mobilization in contradictory ways. Immigrants account for much of the growth among Latinos, and they are the source of potential future booms in electoral clout. But in the short term, they can also be the source of tensions, as evidenced in the differences between the policy preferences of Latino citizens and immigrants. Immigrants also stimulate anti-Latino backlashes, as the "English as the official language" initiatives and Prop. 187 and its progeny illustrate. To be sure, Hispanics unite and mobilize in opposition to such attacks. But when such issues have been put to a vote, Latinos have suffered resounding electoral defeats. The point here is not to blame immigrants for the hypocrisy with which the nation manages its borders or deals with the language rights of its citizens and legal residents. It is, instead, to emphasize that population growth fueled by immigrants affects Latino politics in multiple and contradictory ways.

All of this means that there is no silver bullet with which to transform the Hispanic political arsenal. Instead, Latino political futures are mired in the same muck as the rest of the nation, only deeper. Political parties are failing everybody, not just Latinos. The rules governing campaign finance hurt all but the most affluent, not just Latinos. But because Latinos are still paying the price for past discrimination, as well as experiencing injustices that have the same consequences even if they are not necessarily motivated by the same prejudices, these systemic failures have a particularly negative impact on Hispanics.

There are, it seems, two ways out. The first is to use ethnic appeals to make the potential of Hispanic numbers real. The myopia of such an approach is illustrated by the Proposition 187 vote: Latinos turned out in unprecedented numbers only to be swamped by a counter mobilization of greater proportions. The lesson is clear: if the environment becomes deeply hostile, Latinos can and will respond; but if things get that bad, Latinos will lose.

The second approach is less dramatic but more promising. Latinos must recognize that most of the issues that concern them also affect large segments of the nation. This means that the most effective mid-

and long-term strategies require issue-specific coalitions that cross ethnic boundaries. This is not, it should be emphasized, a "people of color" coalition premised on unspecified cultural and political commonalities. Instead, it is a call for pragmatic, piecemeal efforts designed to achieve concrete objectives—in other words, it's old fashioned politics.

This, then, is the danger of *"el cuento de los números"* and the other fables discussed here. As long as Latino advocates, especially those who are not accountable to Hispanic constituents in any politically meaningful way, feel free to dismiss Latino public opinion and to propagate the false promise that "we can do it on our own," the potential of Hispanic political clout will never be realized.

References

Bean, Frank D., and Marta Tienda. 1987. *The Hispanic Population of the United States*. New York: Russell Sage Foundation.

Brischetto, Robert. 1995. "Voting Patterns Favor GOP but Democratic Support Remains Even," *Hispanic Business*, November, p. 70.

Chávez. Linda. 1991. *Out of the Barrio: Toward a New Politics of Hispanic Assimilation*. New York: Basic Books.

de la Garza, Rodolfo, ed. 1987. *Ignored Voices: Public Opinion Polls and the Latino Community*. Austin: Center for Mexican American Studies, University of Texas at Austin.

de la Garza, Rodolfo O., and Robert R. Brischetto. 1983. "The Mexican American Electorate: Information Sources and Policy Orientations." Austin: Center for Mexican American Studies, University of Texas at Austin.

de la Garza, Rodolfo O., and Louis DeSipio. 1993. "Save the Baby, Change the Bathwater, and Scrub the Tub: Latino Electoral Participation after Seventeen Years of Voting Rights Act Coverage," *University of Texas Law Review* 71 (7): 1479–1539.

de la Garza, Rodolfo O., and Louis DeSipio, eds. 1992. *From Rhetoric to Reality: Latinos in the 1988 Elections*. Boulder, Colo.: Westview.

———. 1996. *Ethnic Ironies: Latino Politics in the 1992 Elections*. Boulder, Colo.: Westview.

de la Garza, Rodolfo O., Louis DeSipio, Angelo Falcón, F. Chris García, and John García. 1992. *Latino Voices: Mexican, Puerto Rican and Cuban Perspectives on American Politics*. Boulder, Colo.: Westview.

de la Garza, Rodolfo, Martha Menchaca, and Louis DeSipio, eds. 1994. *Barrio Ballots: Latino Politics in the 1990 Elections*. Boulder, Colo.: Westview.

de la Garza, Rodolfo O., and Janet Weaver. 1985. "Chicano and Anglo Public Policy Perspectives in San Antonio: Does Ethnicity Make a Difference?" *Social Science Quarterly* 66 (3): 576–86.

DeSipio, Louis. 1996. "Making Citizens or Good Citizens? Naturalization as a Predictor of Organizational and Electoral Behavior among Latino Immigrants," *Hispanic Journal of Behavioral Sciences* 18 (2): 194–213.

Fraga, Luis, Hermán Gallegos, Gerald P. López, Mary Louise Pratt, Renato Rosaldo, José Saldívar, Ramón Saldívar, and Guadalupe Valdés. 1994. *Still Looking for America: Beyond the Latino National Political Survey*. Stanford, Calif.: Stanford Center for Chicano Research, Stanford University.

García, F. Chris, Rodolfo O. de la Garza, John A. García, and Angelo Falcón. n.d. "The Demographic Bases of Latino Party Identification: Ethnicity and Other Partisan Foundations among Mexicans, Puerto Ricans, Cubans and Anglos in the United States." Albuquerque: University of New Mexico.

Guerra, Fernando. 1992. "Conditions Not Met: California Elections and the Latino Community." In *From Rhetoric to Reality: Latino Politics in the 1988 Elections*, edited by Rodolfo O. de la Garza and Louis DeSipio. Boulder, Colo.: Westview.

INS (Immigration and Naturalization Service). 1993. *Statistical Yearbook of the Immigration and Naturalization Service*. Washington, D.C.: U.S. Department of Justice, Immigration and Naturalization Service.

Los Angeles Times. 1983. Latino Poll. Los Angeles, California.

Lubenow, Gerald C., ed. 1991. *California Votes—The 1990 Governor's Race: An Inside Look at the Candidates and Their Campaigns by the People Who Managed Them*. Berkeley, Calif.: Institute of Governmental Studies Press.

McNeely, David. 1996. "Voting Data Proves Hispanics Carried Morales to Victory," *Austin American Statesman*, April 18.

Moreno, Dario, and Christopher L. Warren. 1992. "The Conservative Enclave: Cubans in Florida." In *From Rhetoric to Reality: Latinos in the 1988 Elections*, edited by Rodolfo O. de la Garza and Louis DeSipio. Boulder, Colo.: Westview.

Morris, Celia. 1992. *Storming the Statehouse: Running for Governor with Ann Richards and Dianne Feinstein*. New York: Scribner's Sons.

NALEO (National Association of Latino Elected and Appointed Officials). 1994. *National Roster of Hispanic Elected Officials*. Washington, D.C.: NALEO Education Fund.

Pear, Robert. 1996. "U.S. Strengthens Patrols along the Mexican Border; Acts to Stem Any Spurt in Illegal Immigration," *New YorkTimes*, January 13.

Skerry, Peter. 1993. *Mexican Americans: The Ambivalent Minority*. New York: Free Press.

Southwest Voter Research Institute. 1994. "Record High Latino Vote Provided Feinstein with Margin of Victory." Montebello, Calif.: The Institute, December 16.

Subervi-Vélez, Federico. 1992. "Republican and Democratic Mass Communication Strategies: Targeting the Latino Vote." In *From Rhetoric to Reality: Latinos in the 1988 Elections*, edited by Rodolfo O. de la Garza and Louis DeSipio. Boulder, Colo.: Westview.

Tedin, Kent L., and Richard W. Murray. 1994. "Support for Biracial Political Coalitions among Blacks and Hispanics," *Social Science Quarterly* 75 (4): 772–89.

Tilove, Jonathan. 1996. "Latinos Back Immigration Limits," *San Francisco Examiner*, February 29.

Torres, Joseph. 1995. "Campaign Aims for a Million New Latino Voters in 1996," *Hispanic Link*, October 23.

————. 1996. "Four-State Survey: Latinos Like Affirmative Action, Divided on Immigration," *Hispanic Link*, March 4.

TRC (Tomás Rivera Center). 1995a. "Latinos in Texas: A Socio-demographic Profile." Austin, Tex.: TRC.

————. 1995b. "The Latino Vote at Mid-Decade." Claremont, Calif.: TRC.

————. 1996. "U.S. Hispanic Perspectives." Claremont, Calif.: TRC.

Wilkie, James W. 1973. *Elitelore*. Los Angeles: University of California at Los Angeles.

3

Latinos and Ethnic Politics in California: Participation and Preference

Carole J. Uhlaner

Introduction

Latinos comprise a large and growing portion of the U.S. population and a proportionately larger and even faster growing population segment in California. More than a few commentators have noted that California will almost surely have a "majority minority" population by early in the twenty-first century, with Latinos, African Americans, and Asian Americans collectively outnumbering non-Hispanic whites, and with Latinos the largest of these groups. The role of Latinos in determining California's political future will depend, in part, upon the shape of Latino preferences and participation. Since one-third of the U.S. Latino population lives in California (as of 1988; U.S. Bureau of the Census 1989), national Latino politics reflects politics in California.

Some argue that it is a misnomer to speak of Latino politics. The term "Latino" refers to people who share a Spanish-speaking heritage but are of many different national origins. The designers of the Latino National Political Survey (LNPS) (see de la Garza et al. 1992) have tentatively concluded that—at least for Cuban Americans, Puerto Ricans, and Mexican Americans—the collective label may obscure more than it reveals. On the other hand, political leaders speak about Latino politics (for example, they join the National Association of Latino Elected and Appointed Officials), and certain key issues may well transcend national origin. Since the California Latino population is overwhelmingly of Mexican origin, restricting discussion to Mexican Americans sidesteps the quandary.[1]

However, Mexican Americans differ among themselves in ways that are politically salient. In addition to differences in sociodemographic and political characteristics, the Mexican American population varies in nativity and citizenship. Many Mexican Americans are immigrants; others are the children of immigrants; and others were born into families that have been in the United States for many generations. California has an especially large concentration of immigrants, as it has been a popular destination. For example, 42 percent of immigrants legally admitted in 1989, and 48 percent of those from Mexico and Central and Latin America, intended to live in California (U.S. Bureau of the Census 1991: 11). The usefulness and effectiveness of organizing politics along ethnic lines depend upon whether the interests held in common outweigh these and other differences.

Policy preferences cannot change government outcomes in the absence of participation. Thus we start the discussion of Mexican American politics in California with an examination of political participation. How active are Mexican Americans in comparison with other Californians, both in electoral politics and outside of the electoral sphere? Since any attempt to project future activity must begin by assessing the reasons for any differences, the second task is to understand the general processes that produce activity, both universally and as applied to ethnic politics in California.

On the other hand, participation does not matter unless preferences are different. Thus we next examine preferences, both in terms of partisan identification and in terms of positions on various issues. In what ways do Mexican Americans have common interests, distinctive from those of other Californians?

One specific issue, Proposition 187 in the November 1994 California general election, was widely perceived to be of special importance to Latinos. We conclude with a discussion of that measure and the implications for the future politics of Mexican Americans.

Throughout this chapter, empirical examples will be drawn from several sources of data. First, many of the tables use information from the 1984 "Caltech" study of ethnic minorities in California, funded by the Seaver Institute. This contains separate samples of four California populations: non-Hispanic whites (otherwise referred to below as "Anglos"), African Americans, Latinos, and Asian Americans. There

---

[1] Throughout this chapter, the term Mexican American refers to persons of Mexican national or ethnic origin who reside in the United States, whatever their citizenship, place of birth, or generations of family residence in the United States. The LNPS defines a person as Mexican American as long as he or she, one parent, or two grandparents are of solely Mexican ancestry. Other data used in this chapter rely upon respondents' self-identification as Mexican-origin.

are 574 Latino respondents (of which 513 are Mexican American) and just over 300 in each of the other samples. The samples include both citizens and noncitizens.[2] Second, some of the tables use data drawn from the Latino National Political Study. The LNPS, conducted in 1989–90, sampled U.S. residents (both citizen and noncitizen) of Mexican, Cuban, and Puerto Rican origin. It also sampled non-Latinos living in the areas included in the sampling frame.[3] Since the sampling frame was national, it was not designed to represent residents of specific states. However, in light of the design of the sampling frame, and since California residents make up roughly one-quarter of the 3,415–person sample and are taken from respondents spread over the state, it seems reasonable to use these data as a representation of Californians for Mexican Americans (629 in California) and non-Hispanic whites (133 Anglos in the sample in California). Finally, some tables, especially those addressing Proposition 187, use data from the October 1994 California Field poll (Field Institute 1994).

Participation

Political participation includes any actions taken by individuals in the mass public in an attempt to influence who holds governmental power (via election, for instance) or to influence governmental and other public policy outcomes (for example, by changing the views or actions of those who are in power). While the specific behaviors of political elites such as officeholders, lobbyists, and political organizers are obviously important in producing public outcomes, these full-time players have motivations and take actions that differ substantially from those of most persons, for whom political action is an occasional avocation or rare event.

Voting and Registration

Voting is just one form of political action although a particularly potent one in the aggregate. Votes determine who holds elected power. Though any one individual's vote has very little effect on the outcome in almost any real election, practicing politicians, who face the challenge of getting "their side's" vote out to win elections, use many

---

[2]For details of sample design and nonresponse issues, see Uhlaner, Cain, and Kiewiet 1989; Cain, Kiewiet, and Uhlaner 1991.

[3]See de la Garza et al. 1992 for a fuller discussion of the sample and these data.

TABLE 3.1

ELECTORAL PARTICIPATION BY RACE AND ETHNICITY
(PERCENTAGES)

	1984 "Caltech" California Study Citizens Only				Latino National Political Study, 1989–90 California Residents Only		
	Anglos	African Americans	Mexican Americans	Asian Americans	Anglo Citizens	Mex. Amer. Citizens	Mex. Amer. Noncitizens
Voted in Last Pres. Election	80	81	60	69	78	53	
Now Registered	87	88	72	77	85	67	
Ever Registered					93	77	
Voted for Congress in 1988					72	48	
Voted for Congress in 1986					72	44	
Voted in School Election					47	25	7
N	300	313	356	199	131	263	366

techniques to encourage turnout. A group's voting strength is an indicator of its power. One measure of voting strength is the number of potential voters multiplied by the turnout rate of those who are eligible. Turnout is fairly well defined, but ambiguities in the definition of "potential voter" reflect the legal requirements for voting.

Unlike most other acts of political participation, voting in the United States requires that the participant: (1) be above a certain age, now eighteen years, (2) be a citizen,[4] and (2) be registered.[5] In fact, registration, which is also restricted to citizens, is sufficiently onerous that it is generally included as an act of participation.[6] These requirements produce variation in the count of potential voters depending upon the time horizon. On election day, only registered citizens are potential voters. Several months before the election (that is, before registration has closed), any citizen aged eighteen or over is a potential voter. From the perspective of years, potential voters include youths and noncitizens who have the option of naturalizing. These factors are more important for Mexican American participation than for most other groups in the United States. The population includes large numbers of noncitizens, many of whom have already lived in the United States long enough to qualify for citizenship. As long as substantial immigration continues, and unless rates of naturalization increase, the citizenship requirement will keep the eligible population relatively small. The Mexican American population distribution is also young. A substantial proportion of Mexican Americans (higher than in other ethnic groups) are too young to vote, but the number of Mexican Americans entering eligibility each year exceeds the number leaving (the old cohorts are smaller), resulting in a relatively high growth rate for the eligible population.

How do Latinos compare with other Californians in their rates of electoral participation? Table 3.1 reports voting and registration rates for California citizens from both the 1984 "Caltech" survey and the 1989–90 LNPS survey. The first four columns give the 1984 results, for citizens only, broken out for non-Hispanic whites ("Anglos"), African Americans, Asian Americans, and Mexican Americans. The last three columns give results from the LNPS respondents who live in California, first for Anglos and then for Mexican Americans.

---

[4]There are a few exceptions. The rules for certain local elections permit noncitizens to vote; conversely, noncitizens are theoretically barred from contributing to election campaigns where they can't vote.

[5]Again there are some exceptions: a handful of states permit "registering" at the poll on election day. Rules for registration vary substantially across states and over time. "Motor voter" is a federal law liberalizing registration rules across all states, but implementation has varied from one state to the next.

[6]It also, of course, is available only to citizens above a certain age.

Both sets of data show that voting and registration rates are notably lower for Mexican Americans than for either Anglos or African Americans[7] and somewhat lower than for Asian Americans. If noncitizens are included in the denominator (as in many press reports), the rates for Mexican Americans drop by about 15 points, reflecting only the fact that noncitizens cannot vote.[8] However, comparison of the rates for citizens is more meaningful. The slight differences between Mexican American and Asian American turnout and registration rates suggests a rough equivalence. The differences relative to Anglos and African Americans are large enough to reflect real differences in the translation of numbers into votes, with margins of 15 to 25 points across registration and presidential, congressional, and school elections. On the other hand, these figures do *not* indicate a politically quiescent population. Fully three-quarters of California's Mexican American citizens had been registered to vote at some time, according to the LNPS data, and about half or more voted in various federal elections.

National data suggest that voting rates for non-Hispanic whites and African Americans rose from the early to the mid-1980s and then declined. Latino participation rates began the 1980s at a level well below those of the other two groups, but, according to National Election Study data, they ended the decade near African American rates (Uhlaner n.d.). On the other hand, Current Population Survey data show a fairly constant gap. Elsewhere in the United States, in contrast to California, African American voting and registration rates are below those of non-Hispanic whites. Of course, national Latino rates include persons of various national origins. Cuban Americans are more likely to vote and register than Mexican Americans, while Puerto Ricans have rates similar to the latter group (Uhlaner n.d.).

Different sources of California data disagree as to whether Latino voting participation increased substantially in 1994; in any event it did not decline. Data from the October 1994 California Field poll (Field Institute 1994)[9] indicate that the relative participation rates in

---

[7]The 1984 survey results that California's African Americans vote and register at about the same (or higher) rates than non-Hispanic whites are not aberrant; Field polls and census data (Current Population Survey) show the same thing. Nationwide rates are lower.

[8]Inclusion of noncitizens in the base in the 1984 data produces an apparent turnout rate of 45 percent and registration rate of 55 percent for Mexican Americans and of 48 and 55 percent, respectively, for Asian Americans. It is reasonable to include noncitizens in the base if one is trying to make a point about how much actual influence a population has on election outcomes relative to its size, but such a number is misleading if one is interested in the mechanisms that tend to increase or depress activity.

[9]Percentages reported from the Field poll both here and later in this chapter are calculated using the "nonpolitical" weight provided by the Field Institute; this weight adjusts the sample to match census numbers for age within gender in each of ten re-

California remained much as they were a decade earlier: registration rates in the current election were 91 percent for Anglo citizens (838 cases), 89 percent for African Americans (76 cases), and 76 percent for Latino citizens (Hispanic, Spanish, or Mexican descent) (216 cases). The approximate equality between Anglo and African American rates and the fifteen-point gap for Latino rates mirror the 1984 findings. There is no directly equivalent voter turnout question, but the one that was asked indicates that, among registered voters, Latinos vote less than Anglos or African Americans by amounts consistent with the earlier results.[10] On the other hand, the Southwest Voter Research Institute estimated that the proportion of *registered* Latino citizens who voted in the November 1994 election in California was only slightly below the equivalent figure for the total electorate (57 percent versus 60 percent) and much higher than in the 1990 election (for which they estimate 39 percent) (1995: 1, 3). The Tomás Rivera Center (1996) calculated turnout rates of adult Latino citizens from Current Population Survey data and concluded that these rates were much higher in 1994 than in 1990 and at about the level of 1992. If these conclusions hold up, they suggest an increase in Latino voting rates; the data from the 1980s show about a ten-point gap in turnout among registered voters. The last section of this chapter discusses Proposition 187 as a possible reason for increased participation in California in 1994.

School elections do allow for participation by noncitizens. Here again, Mexican American citizens are less active than Anglos, by about the same margin as in other types of elections. Of note, however, are the 7 percent of noncitizens who take part. As we will see below, despite the legal limitations, noncitizens do participate in politics, more in some activities, less in others.

Because of the barrier that noncitizenship raises to voting, and because of the large numbers of noncitizens among California's Latino residents, the future electoral impact of Latinos will depend in large measure upon the future of naturalization. Especially because substantial numbers of eligible Latino residents have chosen not to naturalize, the political impact of the community could change dramatically in a short time if those numbers change. The decision to

---

gions of the state. The frequencies obtained from the unweighted data are very similar and support identical substantive interpretations.

[10] Only persons currently registered where they live were asked: "Since 1990 there have been six statewide elections in California—[elections listed]. In how many of these six statewide elections did you vote?" Fifty-six percent of Anglos and 50 percent of African Americans said "all six," versus 37 percent of Mexican Americans. Twenty-one percent of Anglos and 31 percent of African Americans said "zero to three," versus 48 percent of Mexican Americans.

naturalize, or not, has many components. Some of these are even extraterritorial, such as changes in Mexican law governing expatriates. Others reflect changes in U.S. laws and policies toward immigrants. In all cases, an increase in citizenship rates increases the pool of potential voters.

However, it is hard to predict the impact that large-scale increases in the number of citizens will have on voting and registration rates. If those Latino noncitizens who are eligible for naturalization are less interested in politics than their already naturalized counterparts but decide to become citizens (for example, because of the current policy threats to noncitizens), then they may participate less and contribute to a reduction in the turnout rate. In other words, these new citizens might produce fewer new voters than anticipated. As it is, foreign-born Latino citizens (that is, the currently naturalized) are significantly less likely to vote or to register than Latinos born in the United States (DeSipio 1996). Even if the current noncitizens were to naturalize and then participate at the same rate as other naturalized citizens, participation *rates* would decline. At the same time, as more Latinos become citizens, the absolute number of participants, and resulting electoral weight, would increase.

Campaigning and Nonelectoral Activities

Political participation includes many activities other than voting and registration. Some actions attempt to influence the way other people vote. For example, people contribute money to candidates or campaigns, display political signs or buttons, help a candidate in a campaign, and attend political rallies or meetings. These electoral activities take place in the context of an election contest but (with the exception of some money contributions) have no legal prerequisites.

Other activities, referred to as "nonelectoral," take place outside the context of elections. These are also intended to affect policy outcomes but without necessarily directly affecting any particular election. Such activities include making one's views known—for example, by contacting a government official or the news media, or signing a petition, or working together with others, such as in a voluntary association or an ad hoc group.[11]

---

[11] Activities that are less conventional and sometimes subject to sanctions or are otherwise risky, such as demonstrations, riots, and strikes, are called political protest. These tend to involve relatively few people. More importantly, the explanations for protest differ from those for conventional participation. Thus political protest activity will not be analyzed here.

Table 3.2 indicates rates for various of these activities, again from the 1984 "Caltech" data and from the LNPS data, separately, for members of different ethnic groups and for citizens and noncitizens. First, consider only the citizens. Although once again Anglos appear more active than Mexican Americans, the differences in activity rates are much more similar across groups for campaign activities than for voting and registering or for the nonelectoral activities. Roughly as many Mexican American citizens as Anglos or African Americans contribute money (despite the big differences in income levels), display campaign stickers, or work on campaigns. All of these acts are fairly infrequent (less than 20 percent participation) in all groups. Once you are dealing with rare forms of participation, each ethnic group has its share of activists.

The nonelectoral activities are more common. Between a quarter and a half of non-Hispanic whites contact the media, a government office, or elected official, or work with others in a community. Differences in percentages between 1984 and the 1989–90 LNPS survey may reflect real changes or the differences in sample design,[12] but most likely they result from variations in question wording. The 1984 data indicate that citizens from all of the other ethnic groups are at least as likely as Anglos to contact the media, and Asian Americans were as likely and African Americans even more likely to work in community groups. Although Mexican American citizens were the least active in community groups, a still substantial one-quarter had worked with one. Anglos were more likely than persons in any of the other groups to contact officials (similar to Verba and Nie's [1972] finding).

Noncitizens are less active than citizens, but they nonetheless show substantial involvement in these nonelectoral activities. In fact, Asian American noncitizens are more likely to contact media than anyone except Asian American citizens, with non–English speakers being the most active. This datum suggests that perhaps they are engaged in home-country politics; the survey neglected to ask about the locus of political activity.

The LNPS data also indicate that Mexican American citizens are less active than Anglos, but the pattern across activities differs from that in 1984. Mexican Americans are relatively more likely to work with a group or attend a meeting and less likely to contact media or sign a petition. Mexican American citizens report less activity than in the 1984 study, with the large exception of contacting a government

---

[12] The 1984 Anglo data are a sample of the state population. Aside from the question of whether the California LNPS respondents can be examined separately, as we are doing here, they are in any case a sample of Anglos who live in areas with at least a 5 percent Latino population. They thus underrepresent those areas of the state with fewer Latino residents.

TABLE 3.2
CAMPAIGN AND NONELECTORAL PARTICIPATION BY RACE, ETHNICITY, AND CITIZENSHIP (PERCENTAGES)

	1984 "Caltech" California Study						Latino National Political Survey California Residents Only		
	Anglo Citizens	Afro Amer. Citizens	Mexican American Citizens	Mexican American Noncitizens	Asian American Citizens	Asian American Noncitizens	Anglo Citizens	Mexican American Citizens	Mexican American Noncitizens
Campaign Activities									
Contribute Money	20	17	14	7	24	6	16	16	1
Display Poster or Sticker; Wear Button	8	10	11	10	4	6	19	17	3
Work on Campaign	6	5	4	1	4	2	5	5	1
Attend Rally, Meeting	15	16	12	4	11	4	12	8	2
Nonelectoral Activities									
Contact Official to Complain or Give Opinion	47	37	29	19	31	20			
Contact Media: Letter to Paper or Magazine	22	20	20	13	25	23			
Contact Gov. Office on Problem or for Info.							39	25	23
Contact Media or Official on Issue							25	14	3
Work with Group on Community Problem	33	38	24	12	32	11	27	20	6
Sign Petition on Issue							57	34	8
Attend Public Meeting							25	20	6
N	300	313	356	137	199	84	131	263	366

office on a problem or for information. About a quarter of Mexican Americans have done this, whether or not they are citizens.

Thus, overall, Mexican American citizens play as much a role in political campaigns at this grassroots level as do Anglos or African Americans. Even noncitizens take part. Mexican Americans are less likely than Anglos to engage in nonelectoral activities, but their absolute rates of participation are high enough to suggest that perhaps every other household has some member who has used these paths to influence.

Why Do Participation Rates Differ?

As shown by a significant body of empirical research, people who participate more in politics tend to have certain characteristics which differ systematically from nonparticipants. Certain racial or ethnic groups may in certain times and places tend to be more or less active than other people, but generally any such differences have less to do with some inherent aspect of sharing that race or ethnicity and more to do with the uneven distribution of the other characteristics, so the association with race and ethnicity is happenstance. This section will first sketch out the general characteristics and assess their importance in accounting for the participation differences already discussed. It then discusses more fully what cross-group differences mean if they reflect random variation, on the one hand, or an essential aspect of the ethnic groups' experiences, on the other.

Repeated studies of political participation in different populations have produced a fair bit of knowledge about the characteristics of participants and nonparticipants (Conway 1991; Verba, Nie, and Kim 1978). First, people with more money and more education are more active, around the world (see, for example, Verba, Nie, and Kim 1978). Second, persons who hold certain attitudes—including interest in politics, a sense of civic duty, a sense of personal efficacy—tend to be more active. (These attitudes are strongly correlated with socio-economic status.) Third, people who are active in voluntary organizations participate more in politics. Fourth, people who identify with political parties are more politically active. In some countries, partisans actually belong to party organizations, which gives an additional boost to activity, but the increase is seen even where party identification is almost purely psychological.

Fifth, certain demographic traits tend to characterize people who are more participatory, in part because of these traits' relationship to attitudes or resources. Older people are more active than the young (because participatory habits develop over time) until they reach very old age (when infirmities restrict activity). People who are more integrated into their communities—the married, homeowners, the residentially stable, people active in organizations—are more active. Historically, men are more active than women; that difference no longer holds in national U.S. voting data, but it does persist for some activities and groups. Other demographic characteristics are of particular relevance to populations with substantial numbers of immigrants. Citizens are more active than noncitizens. English speakers are more active than non–English speakers. Immigrants who have spent more of their lives in the United States and those who have weaker ties to their home country tend to be more active. Language, time in the United States, and ties to home country all may affect the knowledge and salience of U.S. politics for the individual and his or her ability to acquire further information.

Thus, in light of the above general findings, a number of demographic characteristics of the Mexican American population could easily account for its lower rates of participation relative to Anglos and African Americans. First, many Mexican Americans are noncitizens. Among the citizens, many are foreign born and a significant number are more fluent in Spanish than in English. In addition, the Mexican American population is relatively young and has less education and lower income than these other ethnic groups.

Analysis of the 1984 data showed that these factors were in fact sufficient to account for most of the observed differences in participation rates between Mexican American citizens and Anglo citizens for all the electoral and most of the nonelectoral activities (Uhlaner, Cain, and Kiewiet 1989: 207–11).[13] There is one exception: even with other factors controlled, members of all of the minority ethnic groups are still less likely than Anglos to "contact officials."[14] Verba et al. (1993)

---

[13]Six probit estimations were run, with, respectively, register, vote, contribute money, work in groups, contact media, and contact officials as the dependent variable. The independent variables included the demographic factors discussed above plus a set of three variables that took on the value "1" if the respondent was, respectively, Latino, African American, or Asian American. If any of these last three variables differs significantly from zero, that suggests that members of that group are significantly more (if positive) or less (if negative) active than Anglos even after taking into account the differences in demographics. If the variables are zero, then there is no significant difference. Note that Asian Americans were less likely than Anglos to register or vote, even after considering the other variables.

[14]A similar finding with regard to contacting officials was attributed by Verba and Nie (1972) to the social distance between the minority group participant and officials, who are likely to be Anglo. If that explanation is correct, it provides a basis for desiring descriptive representation. Since there are now substantially more non-Anglo officeholders than was the case thirty years ago, the speculation could in principle be tested by matching ethnicity of respondent and the pool of local officials. The numbers are still small enough to make this a difficult and expensive study.

reach a similar conclusion in their analysis of national U.S. data collected in 1989 for the Citizen Participation Study; Latino respondents were substantially less active than Anglo-Whites, but essentially all of the difference could be accounted for by the skewed distribution of "politically relevant resources."

Of course, just because we can identify variables that explain a lower rate of Mexican American participation does not imply that the disparities are acceptable. How are we to interpret the conclusion that most of the difference in participation rates between Mexican Americans and Anglos and African Americans can be accounted for by general factors that happen to be especially prevalent within the Mexican American population? First, political power depends upon actual participation, so lower participation means less power, whatever the cause. Second, even if Mexican Americans are more likely to have characteristics of nonparticipants solely by happenstance, one result is a lower level of electoral mobilization in many Mexican American neighborhoods as candidates concentrate their limited campaign resources on people with more participatory profiles. Third, some of the characteristics that lead to less participation do reflect aspects of the Mexican American ethnic experience. For example, lower education levels are universally associated with lower levels of participation, and Mexican American education levels are lower than Anglos. However, this is not the end of the story. A number of theorists argue that systematic biases in the U.S. educational system limit the attainment of Mexican Americans (for a discussion, see, for example, Gándara's chapter in this volume). Thus, although "controlling for education" does reduce the differences in participation between Mexican Americans and Anglos, the lower educational levels may not be random but instead inherent in the contemporary Mexican American experience. Such cases raise particular concerns about the political and ethical fairness of the resultant disparities.

If the factors that affect participation are themselves integral to a group's political culture or experience, then it is more meaningful to talk about ethnic patterns of participation than if they are distributed by chance. The implications for future levels of activity are far different if the important factors explaining participation are changing or changeable than if they are very stable. Whatever the actual stability of the explanatory factors for Mexican American activity, the conclusion that the identified variables do account for the differences in participation rates removes some mystery. Such putative explanations as "ingrained mistrust" or norms of disengagement are irrelevant and probably wrong (since there is little left to explain). Activists can concentrate on either changing or compensating for more concrete factors, such as noncitizenship, language, education, income, youth, and so forth.

Most of the above variables address the way individuals relate to political life. However, politics also takes place within the context of group identities. Some other factors that increase participation are directly related to group interests and are very much within the purview of political leaders. These are factors that are grounded in the individual's group identity and which, if that identity is politicized, can potentially increase participation. The world contains many persons aspiring to political leadership who take advantage of any opportunity to increase support. A number of theoretical perspectives, including rational actor theory, suggest the importance of leaders in influencing participation rates (see Uhlaner 1989a, 1989b). Ethnic groups can provide, and have in fact provided, effective grounds for mobilization, at least when ethnicity is transformed into group consciousness (see Miller et al. 1981 for a discussion of group consciousness).

The 1984 California data contain several indicators of whether ethnicity provides a basis for mobilization. First, respondents were asked whether they identify issues of special concern to them in terms of their racial or ethnic identity. For those who do, these group interests can serve as a basis for political mobilization, in particular by ethnic leaders. Second, respondents were asked about several forms of discrimination and prejudice directed at members of their group. The experience of discrimination and the perception of prejudice contribute to a sense of group solidarity and shared interests, and thus can also serve as a basis for mobilization.

Enough persons perceive an ethnic problem or prejudice or have experienced discrimination to make these perceptions a potentially important source of activity. Almost half of Mexican Americans (and one-quarter of Anglos, one-third of Asian Americans, and two-thirds of African Americans) do identify some political issue of special concern to their own ethnic, national origin, or racial group (see table 3.3). Substantial numbers have experienced discrimination (one-third of Mexican Americans, half of Asian Americans, two-thirds of African Americans). One-quarter of Mexican Americans believe that people of their national origin receive fewer opportunities than they deserve (a belief shared by only a few Asian Americans and many African Americans). Finally, over half of the members of each group believe that at least some Americans are prejudiced against them. Do these components of ethnic consciousness, perceived group interests, or perceived discrimination increase participation among those who hold them?

The answer, in brief, is yes. Table 3.4 shows the results of probit estimates of the effect upon three forms of electoral participation—registration, voting, and contributing money to a campaign—of these measures of ethnic interests and perceived bias, while also estimating the effects of sociodemographic factors and strength of partisanship. In addition, since group identity may take a nonethnic form, another variable captures respondents who say they identify political problems specific to a nonethnic group that they feel especially part of. Finally, three variables are included that take the value "1" if the respondent is, respectively, Mexican American, African American, or Asian American. The coefficients on these terms indicate how much more or less active members of the group are than Anglos after accounting for the effects of the other variables; a coefficient indistinguishable from zero indicates no difference. In the results reported here, the three measures of bias are added together in a simple scale; the substantive conclusions are the same when they are separated in the estimation.

TABLE 3.3
PERCEPTIONS OF ETHNIC ISSUE, DISCRIMINATION, PREJUDICE,
1984 CALIFORNIA "CALTECH" DATA (PERCENTAGES)

	Anglos	African Americans	Mexican Americans	Asian Americans
Problem of Special Concern to Racial or Ethnic Group	24	65	46	37
Own Group Receives Fewer Opportunities than Deserves	not asked	42	24	9
Respondent Has Personally Experienced Discrimination	not asked	62	36	46
Most Americans Are Prejudiced against Members of Own Group	not asked	17	10	5
Some Americans Are Prejudiced against Members of Own Group	not asked	63	54	52
Most Americans Are Not Prejudiced against Members of Own Group	not asked	21	36	42

TABLE 3.4
PROBIT ESTIMATIONS OF CITIZENS' ELECTORAL PARTICIPATION,
1984 CALIFORNIA "CALTECH" DATA

Independent Variables	Voted in 1984		Registered		Contributed $	
	coeff.[1]	t[2]	coeff.	t	coeff.	t
Mexican American	-0.25	-1.82	-0.20	-1.33	-0.15	-0.99
Black	-0.04	-0.26	-.012	-.072	-0.27	-1.71
Asian American	-0.55	-3.75	-0.59	-3.75	-0.16	-1.06
Age	.038	10.00	.030	7.41	.020	5.33
65 or Older	-0.62	-3.12	-0.35	-1.59	-0.27	-1.56
Some College	0.65	7.01	0.68	6.80	0.45	4.57
Homeowner	0.36	4.22	0.33	3.58	0.38	3.89
Head of Household Unemployed	-0.19	-1.69	-0.12	-0.99	-.093	-0.67
Single Mother	-0.20	-1.41	-.018	-0.12	-0.33	-2.03
Male	-.063	-0.69	-.082	-0.84	0.29	3.01
% of Life Not in U.S.	-.001	-0.50	-.001	-0.40	.004	1.29
Non-English Lang.	-0.26	-2.20	-0.22	-1.75	-0.14	-1.00
Ethnic Problem	.077	0.84	0.15	1.55	0.12	1.19
Nonethnic Identity	0.12	0.85	0.37	2.15	0.27	2.08
Party Strength	0.26	7.87	0.28	8.13	.078	2.12
Perceive Discrimination	0.12	2.29	0.12	2.25	0.10	1.86
Constant	-1.79	-8.47	-1.29	-5.76	-2.56	-10.9
Log Likelihood at Convergence	-566.33		-470.57		-521.87	
N	1,233		1,232		1,225	

[1]Probit coefficients.
[2]T-statistics. Critical value of t for $p < .05 = 1.96$.

The demographic variables have the effects discussed above: older people (except the very old) are more active, as are the better educated, homeowners, and English speakers. Men are more likely to contribute money. Speaking a language other than English lowers voting rates. The political and group interests variables have some effect as well. Strong partisans are more active than those with weak or no party identification. While identifying an issue specific to one's ethnic group has little effect, persons who volunteer some additional politically salient identity are more likely to register and more likely to contribute money than others. And persons who perceive prejudice and discrimination are more likely to be active than those who do not. With these factors considered, Mexican American and African American electoral participation rates are indistinguishable from those of Anglos, although Asian American voting and registration rates are noticeably lower.

Similar analysis of three nonelectoral activities—working in groups, contacting media, and contacting officials—shows similar effects from demographic variables and a stronger effect from the ethnic consciousness variables (table 3.5). The demographic results are essentially the same for working in groups and contacting officials as for the electoral variables. Gender matters for working in groups, with men more active than women.[15] Partisanship is irrelevant for the nonpartisan actions of working in groups or contacting media, but it does go along with increased propensity to contact officials (some of whom are elected). Group interests and discrimination matter. Respondents who have one or more of the components of group consciousness are more active: perceiving a political issue germane to one's ethnicity or having an additional politically relevant identity increases the propensity to work in groups and to contact media or officials. Persons who perceive prejudice or discrimination are more likely to engage in all three acts. Finally, after allowing for all of these factors, there does remain some difference between the participation rates of Anglos and others. Something else is contributing to lower levels of activity for Mexican Americans (and perhaps Asian Americans) when it comes to working in groups, for African Americans in contacting media, and for all in contacting officials.

The effects of each of these factors may differ between ethnic and racial groups. In another analysis (see Uhlaner 1991a) the coefficients on each variable were allowed to vary across ethnic and racial groups and separately for the foreign born and the U.S. born. Most of the effects discussed above are even stronger for Mexican Americans. In particular, those who have spent a higher percentage of their life outside the United States or who do not speak English as a primary language are even less likely to be active than indicated above. The positive impact on nonelectoral activities of ethnic issue consciousness or of having a nonethnic identity is particularly strong for Mexican Americans. There are two deviations: foreign-born renters are as

---

[15] Contacting media is somewhat anomalous, as both age and language are irrelevant. Thus younger persons and non–English speakers are relatively more active than for other types of participation. Further analysis leads to the speculation that a substantial number of respondents are immigrants, especially Asian born, contacting media concerning home country affairs.

likely as homeowners to register or vote, and even very elderly (over age sixty-five) Mexican Americans are more likely than young people to work in groups. Note that since the Mexican American population is young, the net effect of the positive and steep slope on age is to make overall activity rates lower.

TABLE 3.5
PROBIT ESTIMATIONS OF CITIZENS' NONELECTORAL PARTICIPATION,
1984 CALIFORNIA "CALTECH" DATA

Independent Variables	Worked in Group		Contacted Media		Contacted Officials	
	coeff.[1]	t^2	coeff.	t	coeff.	t
Mexican American	-0.29	-2.20	-0.14	-1.02	-0.46	-3.62
Black	-0.21	-1.51	-0.40	-2.63	-0.61	-4.47
Asian American	-0.27	-1.90	.011	.080	-.066	-4.79
Age	.008	2.54	-.003	-0.81	.014	4.34
65 or Older	-0.30	-1.85	.017	.097	-0.25	-1.64
Some College	0.56	6.56	0.39	4.30	0.43	5.21
Homeowner	0.15	1.81	-.041	-0.48	0.20	2.51
Head of Household Unemployed	-.004	-.031	-0.11	-0.93	-0.17	-1.46
Single Mother	.036	0.27	.097	0.72	.061	0.50
Male	0.27	3.10	.087	0.97	-.0005	-.006
% of Life Not in U.S.	-.004	-1.25	-.004	-1.18	-.0012	-0.44
Non-English Lang.	-0.29	-2.31	-0.11	-0.88	-0.35	-2.90
Ethnic Problem	0.31	3.57	0.20	2.18	.085	1.02
Nonethnic Identity	0.37	3.09	0.21	1.69	0.21	1.79
Perceive Discrimination	0.14	2.81	0.13	2.56	0.16	3.37
Party Strength	-.003	-.009	-.009	-0.27	.099	3.18
Constant	-1.44	-7.33	-0.97	-4.85	-1.20	-6.43
Log Likelihood at Convergence	-681.99		-616.29		-735.69	
N	1,232		1,234		1,231	

[1]Probit coefficients.
[2]T-statistics. Critical value of t for p < .05 = 1.96.

Overall, then, the perception of interests based in one's ethnic group and the perception of discrimination and prejudice do contribute to higher levels of political participation, especially for Mexican Americans. This finding has two interesting implications for the ways in which leaders can attempt to mobilize individuals to activity. First, they can appeal to persons who already perceive these interests and then use those perceptions as a basis for ethnic-specific political organization. Second, and perhaps more interesting, they can foster these perceptions in order to increase activity. The process is most straightforward with regard to group interests and often entails simple education. Some of the early campaign discussion of Proposition 187 was directed toward making all Latinos interpret it as relevant to them (because, for example, of the possibilities for generating suspicion and discrimination directed toward citizens as well) rather than just to undocumented residents. Some feminists take pains to argue that, for example, health care and economic growth are women's issues. Perceptions of discrimination are also subject to education. Certain actions may be interpreted by one person as discriminatory and by another as not; leaders can play a role in conceptions of what constitutes appropriate, nondiscriminatory experience. Of course, human history also contains examples of demagogues inflaming feelings of victimization. Perhaps that negative example best makes the point that leaders can influence these perceptions to mobilize activity.

Thus Mexican Americans in California are in fact less likely to participate in politics, across a set of activities, than are Anglos or African Americans, but much of the difference reflects the large number of noncitizens. Mexican American citizens are also somewhat less active than others, but not by huge amounts. The differences that do remain reflect the large number of foreign-born individuals, younger people, and people with relatively low education and income levels. On the other side, partisanship and the perception of group interests increase activity. To the extent that political activity matters because of its contribution to individual development, preferences are irrelevant. However, from a more practical perspective, in which activity matters because of its impact upon outcomes, preferences matter greatly because they determine what the participants are trying to get.

Party and Issue Preferences

We turn now to a consideration of party and issue preferences. If you know a Californian is Mexican American, does that tell you anything about his or her partisanship or position on issues? If it does not, then disparities in participation rates make little difference. Moreover, it may be less meaningful to organize politics on ethnic lines than on some other basis (such as economic class). On the other hand, distinctive views on only a few issues, or even a single one, can sustain ethnic politics if the issues are sufficiently important. If members of several ethnic groups, but not the whole population, agree on some issues, then there is a basis for coalition.

Party Identification

Party identification effectively summarizes many positions. More importantly, it provides a strong clue as to how people will vote. Table 3.6 summarizes data on party identification from the California respondents to the LNPS and from the 1984 "Caltech" survey. These data agree with other sources on the pattern of partisanship. African Americans support the Democrats by a large majority. Anglos are more or less evenly split between supporters of Democrats and of Republicans, while Asian Americans are slightly more Republican than are Anglos.[16] Mexican Americans are clearly more likely to be Democrats than are Anglos, but a substantial minority (maybe a fifth) identify with Republicans, so their support for Democrats is not as overwhelming as that prevailing among African Americans.

More interesting conclusions come from examining the differences in party preference between citizens and noncitizens and between the U.S. born and the foreign born. Not surprisingly, noncitizens are much more likely to respond "don't know" to the question on party identification than are citizens. Mexican American noncitizens who do respond are more likely than citizens to be independents, a bit more likely to support Republicans, and much less likely to consider themselves Democrats. Nonetheless, they still are more likely than Anglos to identify with Democrats. Foreign-born Mexican American citizens are also more likely to support Republicans (by ten points) than the U.S. born. Among Asian Americans, the foreign born are also more likely to support Republicans than the U.S. born, but by a smaller margin than for Mexican Americans and with no difference by naturalization status.

Analysis reported elsewhere (Cain, Kiewiet, and Uhlaner 1991) suggests that the difference between native-born and immigrant partisanship among Asian Americans is the result of a composition effect:

---

[16]I separated Asian Americans by national origin, but there are not really enough cases for analysis, so the following should be taken as suggestive only. The Filipinos and Japanese Americans are split more or less evenly between the two parties, while Americans of Chinese, Korean, and Vietnamese national origin are more likely to identify with Republicans. Republican identification is strongest among persons who give a hard-line answer on defense issues, supporting a speculation that foreign policy preferences strongly influence these party choices.

TABLE 3.6
PARTISAN PREFERENCES BY RACE, ETHNICITY, AND CITIZENSHIP
AS % OF THOSE WITH A PREFERENCE

Latino National Political Survey			
	Democrat	Independent[1]	Republican	No Answer
Anglo Citizens	35	29	36	1
Mexican American Citizens	62	24	14	5
Mexican American Noncitizens	46	31	23	33

1984 "Caltech" California Survey			
	Democrat	Independent[1]	Republican	No Answer
Anglo Citizens	38	28	34	9
African American Citizens	77	19	4	5
Asian Americans				
All Citizens	35	29	36	12
All Foreign-born	32	24	43	21
Foreign-born Citizens Only	33	25	42	14
Mexican Americans				
All Citizens	60	23	17	10
All U.S.-born	60	24	15	11
All Foreign-born	48	27	25	20
Foreign-born Citizens Only	60	15	25	7
Noncitizens	43	32	25	24

[1]Independents include leaners and those few who identify with a party other than Democrats or Republicans.

recent immigrants have come disproportionately from countries whose residents prefer Republicans, once in the United States, for foreign policy reasons. Mexican Americans' partisanship seems instead to reflect a learning process; support for Democrats increases with time in the United States and in subsequent generations. If the party system remains stable, one could thus expect increasing support for Democrats as current Mexican American immigrants naturalize and have U.S.–born children.[17]

---

[17] This assumes stable or slowing immigration.

Issue Preferences

Partisanship provides a very broad-brush picture of preference which may obscure substantial agreement or disagreement on specific issues. But some issues weigh more heavily than others. This fact complicates any assessment of the extent of policy agreement among people. Nonetheless, we make an attempt to situate Mexican Americans among other Californians with regard to a set of issues asked in the 1984 "Caltech" study. Recall that these issues were important at the time. While some specific items have faded in salience, they can still serve as indicators of underlying attitudes.

There are several caveats in using these data to interpret policy positions. First, ethnicity may not be relevant or, if relevant, not the most important or the only dimension for differentiating preference. Persons within an ethnic group may differ more from each other than from those in different groups when other characteristics, such as economic class, immigration status, and so forth, affect preference. Thus we need to consider these other characteristics of respondents, not just their ethnic or racial group, in assessing opinions. Second, since few members of the public care much about issues, most persons can be swayed on many points, and sometimes leaders have an incentive to try to sway them. Third, survey responses frequently do not reflect considered opinions. Thus the preferences reported here provide a fuzzy snapshot, frozen in time, of a malleable situation; they should not be overinterpreted. They provide a sense of commonality of views across groups of people but not a definitive picture of policy positions.

Thirteen issues were tapped, covering "guns," "butter," a number of social issues, two bilingual issues, and two points relating to immigration (respondents were interviewed before passage of the Immigration Reform and Control Act of 1986).[18] Table 3.7 gives a simple tabulation of the percentage in each ethnic or racial category saying they take the "support" side on each issue, after excluding those respondents who had no opinion. Asian American and Mexican American respondents are separated into U.S. born and foreign born.

Compared with Anglos, U.S.–born Mexican Americans tend to take more "liberal" views on a number of issues—supporting welfare spending and the ERA and opposing the death penalty. These results

---

[18] The issues, with answers coded as "support/oppose," include increased spending on defense, increased spending on welfare, amnesty for undocumented aliens, employer sanctions for those hiring undocumented workers, bilingual education, bilingual ballots, the Equal Rights Amendment, tax credits for private schools, prayer in school, a ban on abortion funding, gun control, the death penalty, and a pro-choice position on abortion.

are consistent with LNPS data that show Mexican Americans nationally more than twice as supportive as Anglos of programs to help African Americans (de la Garza et al. 1992: 91). Mexican Americans are more "conservative" in their support for prayer in schools and their opposition to abortion. And they are substantially more supportive of amnesty and bilingual ballots and education and more opposed to employer sanctions. On all these issues, the foreign born hold views in the same direction, but even more so. On the remaining issues—defense spending, private school tax credit, a ban on abortion funding, and gun control—there is little difference between Anglos and Mexican Americans.

TABLE 3.7
ISSUE PREFERENCES BY RACE, ETHNICITY, AND NATIVITY,
1984 "CALTECH" CALIFORNIA SURVEY
(NUMBER IN FAVOR AS % OF THOSE WITH AN OPINION)

	Anglos	African Americans	Mexican Americans U.S.-born	Mexican Americans Foreign-born	Asian Americans U.S.-born	Asian Americans Foreign-born
Increase Defense $	36	26	36	38	36	55
Increase Welfare $	67	93	79	86	75	71
Amnesty	53	54	66	86	55	57
Employer Sanctions	70	62	55	41	74	51
Bilingual Education	46	71	73	79	49	61
Bilingual Ballots	30	56	63	71	38	52
Support ERA	78	93	86	93	84	84
Private School Tax Credit	55	53	50	55	45	56
Prayer in Schools	55	74	62	76	51	62
Ban Abortion Funding	42	47	40	42	27	48
Gun Control	51	50	55	54	54	69
Death Penalty	83	61	78	64	89	81
Pro-Choice	61	47	44	34	63	47

African Americans are more supportive than Mexican Americans of increasing welfare spending and more opposed to increasing defense spending, more or less share the views of Anglos on the two immigration issues, and are the least supportive of the death penalty. On bilingual education and ballots, ERA, prayer in schools, and abortion, African Americans' preferences resemble those of Mexican Americans, while all three groups are equally split on gun control and aid to parochial schools. Preferences on a number of issues differ by place of birth for Asian Americans. U.S.–born Asian Americans closely resemble Anglos in their views on the immigration and bilingualism issues, while the foreign born resemble the U.S.–born Mexican Americans. The U.S. born adopt the most pro-choice positions. The foreign born stand out in their support for increased defense spending.

Overall, Mexican Americans hold somewhat liberal views, with nativity having effects in the predictable direction. The minority groups agree on enough issues that skillful leaders could perhaps weld a coalition, but the areas of disagreement—such as immigration and defense and welfare spending—make a coalition far from inevitable.

To examine intergroup agreement systematically, probit estimations (not shown here) were run to assess whether the differences in position among African Americans, Asian Americans, and Mexican Americans are statistically significant (see Uhlaner 1991b). Anglos were excluded from the analyses. Each estimation had as the dependent variable the percentage of respondents supporting one of the issues, with six independent variables: U.S.–born Mexican Americans, foreign-born Mexican American citizens, foreign-born Mexican American noncitizens, and the same three categories for Asian Americans. African Americans are more supportive of welfare and want to spend less on defense than any of the groups in the Mexican or Asian American categories. There are few differences on the social issues.[19] The positions on immigration and language issues do differ. All of the noncitizens oppose employer sanctions and support bilingual ballots more than African Americans. Mexican Americans, whatever their citizenship status or nativity, support amnesty more than either African Americans or Asian Americans. Support for bilingual education is about the same among Mexican American citizens, African Americans, and Asian American noncitizens.[20] Mexican

---

[19] Foreign-born Asians support gun control more, African Americans and noncitizen Mexican Americans oppose the death penalty more, and Asian American citizens and U.S.–born Mexican Americans show less support for the ERA.

[20] The few points difference observed in table 3.7 do not translate into statistically significant differences in the probit estimation. Whether or not a difference is statisti-

American noncitizens are significantly more supportive while Asian American citizens are significantly less supportive, both of bilingual education and of bilingual ballots. The position of Asian American noncitizens presumably reflects self-interest. These data do not let us assess why African Americans are supportive of Latinos on language issues, especially bilingual education. Perhaps they sympathize with those who are oppressed (but the one test available in these data fails to support that hypothesis[21]). Perhaps they see bilingual education as something that will improve schools, which they frequently share with Latinos.

Race and ethnicity are not the only characteristics that influence positions on issues. Overall differences in opinion may reflect differences in the distribution of such characteristics as income and education, or differences in the perception of life chances or the experience of discrimination. If preference on an issue appears similar after considering these factors, it does not change different percentages of support in each group for that issue. It does, however, suggest that people who share the characteristic across groups are more similar in their views than people within the group who differ on it, suggesting alternative possibilities for political organizing. In other cases, where preference differences are accentuated by controls, differences in the distribution of other factors may mask ethnic or racially specific preferences. Table 3.8 shows results of probit analyses similar to those described above with the addition of variables measuring language, religion (Catholic or evangelical Protestant), gender, homeownership, education, party preference, personal experience of discrimination, and perception that African Americans or Latinos have fewer opportunities than they deserve. These last variables are separated by whether or not the respondent is African American or Mexican American. The table reports all of the coefficients for the basic ethnicity, citizenship, and nativity variables but only reports other variables if they are (almost) statistically significant (t-values above 1.7 or so).

The introduced variables are sufficient to explain some of the differences attributed above to ethnicity, nativity, or citizenship. Consider first the "guns," "butter," immigration, and language issues. Except for the amnesty issue, the distinctive positions of noncitizen Mexican Americans can be accounted for by these other factors, as can the positions of the noncitizen Asian Americans on welfare and bilingual ballots, the greater support among U.S.–born Mexican

---

cally significant depends in part upon the number of cases in the category (as this affects the variance).

[21] Those who see Latinos as receiving fewer opportunities than they deserve are less supportive of bilingual education, contradicting that hypothesis.

TABLE 3.8
ISSUE PREFERENCES OF NON-ANGLOS BY ETHNICITY, CITIZENSHIP, AND NATIVITY,
CONTROLLING FOR POLITICAL AND DEMOGRAPHIC FACTORS[1]

	Increase Arms $	Increase Welfare $	Amnesty	Employer Sanctions	Bilingual Education	Bilingual Ballots
Noncitizen Mexican	-.17[2] (-.92)[3]	-2.9 (-1.48)	1.18 (6.68)	-.33 (-1.81)	-.19 (-1.08)	-.08 (-.42)
Noncitizen Asian	.41 (2.03)	-.43 (-1.90)	.21 (1.18)	-.44 (-2.12)	-.15 (-.75)	.05 (.23)
Foreign-born Mexican Citizen	.07 (.31)	-.51 (-2.06)	.64 (2.83)	-.06 (-.26)	-.47 (-2.15)	-.24 (-1.05)
Foreign-born Asian Citizen	.53 (2.70)	-.99 (-5.04)	-.04 (-.21)	.05 (.25)	-.72 (-4.28)	-.71 (-3.94)
U.S.-born Mexican	.04 (.30)	-.64 (-4.21)	.31 (2.67)	-.08 (-.67)	-.32 (-2.45)	-.19 (-1.47)
U.S.-born Asian	.05 (.29)	-.63 (-3.34)	.03 (.18)	.30 (1.86)	-.64 (-4.05)	-.56 (-3.64)
Blacks Have Fewer Chances	-.37 (-2.91)					
Blacks x Blacks Have Fewer Chances						
Latinos Have Fewer Chances	.34 (2.59)					

	(1)	(2)	(3)	(4)	(5)	(6)
Mexicans x Latinos Fewer Chances					.53 (3.06)	.40 (2.58)
Non-Mexicans x Latinos Fewer Chances						
Discrimination Experience	-.12 (-2.29)				-.12 (-2.35)	
English Not Language				-.24 (-2.00)		.22 (1.83)
Catholic						
Evan. Protestant						
Male	.16 (1.67)					
Homeowner		-.29 (-2.70)			-.21 (-2.19)	
Education (years)	-.06 (-2.76)	.30 (4.74)		.05 (2.92)	-.06 (-3.23)	-.04 (-2.31)
Age					-.02 (-5.76)	-.016 (-5.77)
Party (Democrat Positive)	-.23 (-3.79)					
Constant	.55 (1.77)	1.53 (10.39)	.09 (1.11)	-.41 (-1.59)	2.54 (7.41)	1.45 (4.66)
Log Likelihood at Convergence	-496	-394	-516	-580	-545	-603
N	812	965	837	885	974	962

	Support ERA	Tax Credit for Private Schools	Prayer in School	Ban Abortion Funding	Gun Control	Death Penalty	Pro-Choice
Noncitizen Mexican	-.17 (-.69)	-.13 (-.69)	.53 (2.97)	.15 (.86)	-.13 (-.70)	-.37 (-2.07)	.02 (.14)
Noncitizen Asian	-.01 (-.04)	.22 (1.06)	.11 (.59)	.22 (1.04)	.49 (2.20)	.20 (1.06)	-.40 (-2.24)
Foreign-born Mexican Citizen	-.51 (-1.75)	.20 (.84)	.30 (1.33)	.25 (1.12)	-.10 (-.46)	.27 (1.06)	.33 (1.56)
Foreign-born Asian Citizen	-.50 (-2.33)	-.23 (-1.23)	-.02 (-.09)	.13 (.71)	.22 (1.09)	.75 (3.74)	-.18 (-1.10)
U.S.-born Mexican	-.61 (-3.46)	-.19 (-1.19)	.05 (.36)	.09 (.62)	-.04 (-.31)	.22 (1.47)	.00 (.04)
U.S.-born Asian	-.32 (-1.54)	-.29 (-1.62)	-.30 (-1.70)	-.43 (-2.34)	.12 (.66)	.89 (4.60)	.02 (.15)
Blacks Have Fewer Chances		-.30 (-1.83)					.17 (1.87)
Blacks x Blacks Have Fewer Chances					-.34 (-2.09)		
Latinos Have Fewer Chances				-.23 (-2.07)			
Mexicans x Latinos Have Fewer Chances							
Non-Mexicans x Latinos Fewer Chances						-.36 (-2.33)	

	(1)	(2)	(3)	(4)	(5)	(6)	(7)
Discrimination Experience	.40 (2.85)	.20 (1.81)			.27 (2.36)		
English Not Language							-.25 (-1.98)
Catholic						.29 (2.39)	-.34 (-3.23)
Evan. Protestant			.59 (4.17)	.30 (2.23)			
Male					-.42 (-4.83)	.26 (2.70)	
Homeowner		-.17 (-1.77)				.18 (1.81)	
Education (years)	-.05 (-1.84)	.04 (2.16)		.05 (2.30)			.07 (4.13)
Age		.013 (4.33)	.012 (4.17)	.009 (3.20)			-.007 (-2.83)
Party (Democrat Positive)	.18 (2.59)				.10 (1.72)		
Constant	1.92 (5.27)	-.88 (-2.54)	-.19 (-1.17)	-1.20 (-3.48)	.23 (1.88)	.12 (.97)	-.35 (-1.16)
Log Likelihood at Convergence	-305	-556	-518	-540	-601	-468	-696
N	917	830	864	820	916	870	1,055

[1] Estimation excludes Anglos. Ethnic coefficients give effects relative to African Americans.
[2] Probit coefficient.
[3] t-statistic.

Americans for defense spending, and the support among U.S.–born Asian Americans for employer sanctions. On the other hand, once one controls for these sociodemographic and political variables, Mexican American citizens are less likely than African Americans or noncitizens to support bilingual education. Otherwise, relative positions on these six issues are unaffected by the controls; for example, Mexican American and Asian American citizens are still less supportive of welfare spending than African Americans, even taking account of everything else.

The control variables tend to further weaken the effect of the ethnic, nativity, and citizenship variables on the social issues. Distinctions between African Americans and others on prayer in school disappear once one controls for age and evangelical Protestant religious affiliation; after accounting for these factors, noncitizen Mexican Americans appear among the most supportive of school prayer. There is a similar shift for the death penalty issue. After accounting for other characteristics, the opinions of Mexican American citizens differ little from those of African Americans, and noncitizen Mexican Americans are more strongly opposed. There are a few other shifts.[22] Overall, especially on the issues most closely tied to ethnicity and citizenship, some cross-group differences of opinion transcend differences in sociodemographic characteristics.

To summarize: Mexican Americans in California are moderately participatory. The large number of noncitizens, of naturalized citizens, of young people, and of people with lower income and education levels accounts for most of the differences in activity rates between Mexican Americans and Anglo Californians. On party and issue preferences, Mexican Americans share some commonalities with African Americans. On a number of issues, however, the differences among Mexican Americans—based on, for instance, citizenship status—exceed those between racial and ethnic groups. Thus, while political organization on ethnic lines and coalition formation across ethnic and racial groups are potentially feasible, dissensus, both within and across groups, has a strong basis.[23] Those who wish to

---

[22] Foreign-born Asian American citizens are no longer distinguishable from African Americans in their level of support for gun control, nor are U.S.–born Asian American citizens distinguishable in their stance on the ERA. On the other hand, after respondents are matched on religion, age, and education, noncitizen Asian Americans appear significantly more anti-abortion than African Americans.

[23] In the first-past-the-post electoral systems ubiquitous in the United States, geography can inhibit or promote the ethnic definition of interests. Ethnic groups whose members are sufficiently geographically concentrated to provide a swing bloc or potential majority in a district have an opportunity to elect persons from the group, and thus achieve descriptive representation. They also provide an apparently irresistible target for politicians who hope to be elected. Those who belong to the group thus have an interest in promoting an ethnic political identity and enhancing activity.

promote Latino interests must contend with the reality that leaders cannot always readily locate those interests. Sometimes, however, they appear clearly, as in California's November 1994 statewide election. We turn now to a brief discussion of participation and preference with respect to recent laws directed toward immigrants.

Participation and Preference in the Wake of Prop. 187

Proposition 187 was passed in the November 1994 California election. Although various of its provisions are under litigation, the initiative as passed makes undocumented immigrants ineligible for public social services, public health care, or public schooling, except in certain emergencies. It places the enforcement onus on public employees, who are required to assess whether services should be denied under terms of the proposition and to report anyone suspected of being in the country illegally. The November 1994 election also shifted control of the U.S. Congress, which has subsequently been considering legislation that limits services for both legal and illegal immigrants.

Neither Proposition 187 nor other proposed legislation specifically names any national origin or ethnic group. However, the large proportion of immigrants within the Latino population and the large proportion of Latinos among recent immigrants, both documented and undocumented, have led many observers to identify a Latino interest.[24] More precisely, since Puerto Ricans have U.S. citizenship and since Cubans are admitted under special refugee provisions, Mexican Americans and the smaller populations of Central and South American immigrants are seen as particularly affected. Such legislation seems to provide plausible ground for issue-based mobilization. Does there in fact exist a common interest, distinct from that of people of other racial and ethnic groups? Has it served as a basis for mobilization? How might it affect future politics? In offering a preliminary assessment, we can illuminate some of the themes of participation and preference discussed above and address prospects for future action.

Although Proposition 187 addresses the treatment of undocumented immigrants, one could, and many did, argue that it would

---

[24] The California Asian American population also includes many immigrants. Discussion of Proposition 187 focused less upon Asian Americans for several reasons. First, the overall population is much smaller. Second, it is perceived as having fewer undocumented immigrants, absolutely and proportionately, both among Asian Americans and among the total population of undocumented immigrants. Third, the population has many fewer noncitizens eligible for citizenship; in contrast to Mexican Americans, Asian American legal immigrants typically naturalize as soon as they can.

have a negative impact upon all Latinos. Service providers, who are charged with denying services to the ineligible, would, it was argued, err on the side of denying services to all Latinos, even U.S.–born citizens, or at the very least put them in the uncomfortable position of needing continually to prove eligibility. The result would be inconvenience at best and discrimination at worst. Under this argument, all Latinos share an interest. On the other hand, the provisions apply only to the undocumented, not to citizens or legal residents who therefore may have different interests and preferences than undocumented residents. As many Mexican Americans as Anglos agree, nationwide, that "there are too many immigrants" (de la Garza et al. 1992: 101). (However, many more Mexican Americans than Anglos— 41 percent versus 16 percent—support programs to help refugees and legal immigrants; see de la Garza et al. 1992: 91.)

If one allows for the difficulties of distinguishing among noncitizens in a survey according to their legal status, and for the likelihood that noncitizens, even if legal residents, may have a larger number of undocumented friends and family, then interests may differ as well between citizens and noncitizens. An even greater source of a split between citizens and noncitizens comes from the general anti-immigration tone of the campaign and explicit content of later measures (for example, provisions of the Republicans' Contract with America). Since interpretation of Proposition 187 was not only ambiguous but also heavily dependent on how it was tied into other policies and specific campaigns (where candidates staked out positions as proponents or opponents), the opinions of ordinary people would have been especially prone to shifting as they learned more and as the campaign progressed.

Thus the data from the October 21–30, 1994, California Field Poll Study (summarized in table 3.9), provide a time-limited glimpse of preferences on Proposition 187 as of a week or two before the election. Note that while most respondents had heard about Proposition 187, an extraordinary 98 percent of Mexican American noncitizens had done so. When only those respondents who had heard something about the proposition were asked, these noncitizens also opposed it overwhelmingly (97 percent "no," with none undecided). Mexican American citizens, however, are not as distinctive; just over half opposed Prop. 187 and a third supported it, with the rest undecided. These distributions are similar to those for African Americans. Anglo citizens are more supportive of Prop. 187 than the Mexican American citizens (half supported the measure) by a clear, but not overwhelming, margin.

Thus ethnicity matters, in the sense that Anglos are distinctive from either African Americans or Mexican Americans, but the absence of citizenship matters even more. Note that there is essentially

TABLE 3.9
POSITION ON PROPOSITION 187 BY RACE OR ETHNICITY (PERCENTAGES)

	Anglo Citizens	African American Citizens	Mexican American Citizens	Mexican American Noncitizens
% Know about				
Prop. 187	90	86	89	98
N for These %s	841	77	218	110
Of respondents who know, those who plan to vote:				
Yes	50	41	32	3
Undecided	16	15	13	0
No	34	45	55	97
% Very Certain				
of "Yes" Voters	78	73	79	84
of "No" Voters	72	72	79	78
N for These %s	769	67	195	107
Prop. 187 summarized in question for all respondents.				
Position after summary:				
Yes	55	55	39	4
Undecided	8	4	7	2
No	37	42	54	93
N for These %s	841	77	218	110
Position after summary for respondents who knew before:				
Yes	55	51	36	4
Undecided	8	4	7	2
No	37	45	57	95
N for These %s	769	67	195	107
Position after summary of respondents who did not know:				
Yes	53	74	59	29
Undecided	11	0	6	32
No	36	26	35	39
N for These %s	72	10	23	3
Care if Prop. 187 Passes				
A Great Deal	59	59	67	71
Somewhat	31	26	24	12
Only a Little or				
Not at All	9	15	9	18
N for These %s	815	72	211	106

Source: California Field Poll Study, October 21–30, 1994.

no difference across groups in the high degree of certainty respondents expressed that they would stick to their planned vote. More surprising, at least to this author, is the fairly small margin by which Mexican Americans cared more than Anglos or African Americans whether the proposition passed. Mexican American noncitizens do have the highest proportion of persons who care a great deal, but also of those who care only a little or not at all. The Field poll also asked all respondents their position on Proposition 187 after offering them a capsule summary of its provisions. Both Mexican American citizens and African Americans who had not heard about the proposition are substantially more supportive of it than those citizens who had heard of it, bringing the overall distributions of opinion closer to those for Anglos.

These data indicate a clearly distinctive interest for noncitizen Mexican Americans based upon Proposition 187. That virtually all of the noncitizens, who are otherwise relatively uninvolved in politics, had heard about Proposition 187 and had taken the position that an outside observer would consider consistent with their interests is a remarkable testament to the rationality of ordinary people in political life when confronted with an issue that matters. Mexican American citizens were split in their views in proportions closer to California citizens of other ethnicities and races than to noncitizen Mexican Americans. That split mirrors real differences in interests. Extrapolating from these findings and the 1984 issue data, one might expect that there was an even greater split in opinion between citizen and noncitizen Asian Americans.[25]

Thus, in answer to the first question, as of October 1994 Proposition 187 galvanized a common interest among *noncitizen* Mexican Americans, but a substantial minority of Mexican American *citizens* held the opposite view, raising a question about the extent of shared interest. On the other hand, exit poll data indicate that Latinos voted against Proposition 187 by 73 to 27 percent, versus 52 to 48 percent of African Americans and Asian Americans in favor of it and 64 percent of Anglos voting yes (Field Institute 1995: 5),[26] so the issue clearly created a cleavage between Latino and other voters. How can one reconcile the 55 to 32 percent in favor of a "no" vote among Mexican American citizens in the October survey with the 73 versus 27 percent opposition in the exit poll? First, opinions may, in fact, have changed in the last week or two of the campaign as both voters and the media

---

[25] Unfortunately, there were too few Asian American respondents for analysis.

[26] The Field Institute derived these numbers by averaging the Voter News Service (N=3,050) and *Los Angeles Times* (N=5,336) exit poll results. They do not break down the Latino category by national origin.

paid even more attention to the election. Note that if the 13 percent undecided all shift to the "no" side, the distribution becomes essentially identical (well within sampling error) to the exit poll results. If that is the case, then citizen and noncitizen opinions were closer than suggested by the October poll, supporting the possibility of joint mobilization around related issues. Second, opinions may not have shifted, but the opponents of Proposition 187 may have been more likely to vote than its supporters.[27] Exit polls, by design, only tap the opinions of those who voted; when turnout is around 50 percent, there is a lot of room for voters' opinions to differ from the whole population's. If this is the case, the issue may serve to rally politically involved Mexican Americans but not to mobilize previously inactive citizens. For purposes of political leadership, it may well be sufficient to have an issue that produces common ground across the most active citizenry. Are 32 percent, or 27 percent for that matter, on the other side enough to "matter"? The answer to that will more likely come out of practical politics than theory.

Proposition 187 could in any case have contributed to greater electoral participation, on both sides. Three-quarters of Mexican Americans who opposed the proposition cared a great deal if it passed; about the same proportion of Anglo and African American *supporters* cared a great deal. Conversely, two-thirds of Mexican American citizen supporters and just under 60 percent of opponents from the other two groups cared a great deal.[28] A number of Latino leaders have argued that mobilization did occur. The Southwest Voter Research Institute (1995) reported an increase in turnout among *registered* Latinos from 39.1 percent in 1990, the most recent previous off-year election, to 56.6 percent in 1994, compared with rates for Anglos of 58.6 percent in 1990 and 60.4 percent in 1994. They attribute the large relative increase in Latino participation to opposition to Prop. 187. Since these figures only count turnout among those who are registered, they are not completely comparable with other figures cited in this chapter (as registration rates may themselves have changed). However, the Tomás Rivera Center reaches a similar conclusion from analysis of Current Population Survey data on the number of citizens voting in 1994 (Tomás Rivera Center 1996). They calculate that 45.7 percent of adult Latino citizens in California voted in November 1994,

---

[27] Note that if only the "undecideds" stayed home, the "no to yes" ratio would have been about 62 to 38. If all of the undecideds did stay home, then a turnout rate of 40 percent among the supporters and 60 percent among the opponents of the proposition would be sufficient to produce the 73 to 27 split among voters against the proposition.

[28] People like to say they care a great deal; 40 to 50 percent of those undecided on the proposition said they cared a great deal about the outcome.

up from 36.7 percent in 1990 (the preceding midterm election) and down only a hair from the 45.8 percent voting in 1992, the preceding presidential election year. In contrast, in the other eight states with large Latino populations that they examine, one sees the more usual pattern of a substantial drop in participation from the presidential (1992) to the off-year (1994) election, with 1994 rates at or below 1990 levels. They attribute the increased turnout to the importance in the campaign of "issues that targeted Latinos" (Tomás Rivera Center 1996: 12), including not just Proposition 187 itself but also senatorial and gubernatorial campaigns in which it played a prominent role. On the other hand, based on exit polls, the *Los Angeles Times* claimed that Proposition 187 had no discernible effect on turnout. Most of the evidence suggests that Proposition 187 probably did serve as a basis for mobilization in November 1994, and thus the answer to the second question is a qualified yes.

The longer-run impact on mobilization is more interesting. The issue has remained salient. Services for immigrants, both legal and illegal, have remained a prominent part of policy discussion, in part because Proposition 187 passed. Other proposals touch more general attitudes and policies concerning immigration. Leaders will likely have plenty of time and opportunity to use these issues to encourage activity. To the extent that Mexican American citizens are split in their opinions, the issue can possibly be divisive and at best useful for organizing only part of the community. But if policies increasingly target legal immigrants as well, or lead to discrimination against all Latinos, these issues are more likely to galvanize broad-based opposition.

Perhaps the most interesting and most likely consequence of Proposition 187 and related proposals is increased power for Mexican Americans through increased rates of naturalization. Many studies have found that large portions of Latino immigrants eligible for citizenship do not naturalize. For example, the NALEO Educational Fund (1992) reported, from a 1988 national sample, that half of Latino immigrants who had been in the United States from five to nineteen years had not begun the naturalization process; of those who had been in the United States over twenty years, more than a quarter had not begun, and another quarter had begun but not completed, the process.

The 1986 Immigration Reform and Control Act (IRCA) provided one boost to naturalization by increasing the pool of eligible persons. The recent policy climate has provided a push. In fact, since passage of Prop. 187, citizenship applications have risen dramatically. Applications in Los Angeles rose by a factor of five from 1994 to 1995 (McDonnell 1995). Anecdotal evidence suggests that applicants are reacting directly to the proposed cuts in services to immigrants and to fears of future changes (see, for example, Verhovek 1995). The clearest outcome of the chilling climate for immigrants is to transform them into citizens—that is, into potential voters.

Conclusion

Latinos make up about a quarter of California's population but just over 10 percent of the voting electorate (Southwest Voter Research Institute 1995). Their numbers and potential power thus exceed their current political weight. Citizenship—or, to be more precise, its absence—is by far the most important limitation on Mexican American political participation. Among citizens, lower levels of income and education, the large proportion of young people, and the substantial numbers with limited facility in English contribute to lower participation rates, but these differences in activity are relatively modest by comparison with the impact of citizenship. Thus, assessing the future of naturalization and immigration provides the key to predicting the political future of Latinos in the state.

If future patterns of issue preference resemble past patterns, Latinos will continue to add to support for generally liberal policies, by comparison with the positions of Anglos and Asian Americans. If partisan preferences follow past patterns, the Democrats will get more support than the Republicans, although not as overwhelmingly as from African Americans. Some issues that are popularly labeled Latino issues, such as those concerning immigration and language policies, do evoke more support from Mexican Americans than from people of other race or ethnicity. However, on many of these issues noncitizens or the foreign born hold distinctive positions which differ from those of citizens or the U.S. born. On the other hand, some coalition may be feasible. African Americans are just as supportive as Latinos of the "Latino" position on some issues—bilingual education—and fall between Latinos and Anglos on others—employer sanctions and bilingual ballots. Status as noncitizen transcends differences in national origin in producing commonality on some issues, such as employer sanctions and bilingual education.

As passage of Proposition 187 and its aftermath have shown, some issues that appear to be specific to a subset of immigrants, and that currently split opinion within the Mexican American community, nonetheless have the potential to be perceived as of general salience to all Latinos and could serve as a basis for political mobilization. The future of such issues depends in part upon communication—for example, how effectively leaders opposed to Proposition 187 can convince U.S.–born Latinos that their interests dictate a "no" vote on this and related measures. In part it depends upon the results; if implementation of Proposition 187 does increase discrimination against

Latinos, a shared interest becomes more obvious. As legislation targets legal immigrants, the shared interest grows. The national debate on immigration legislation that went on for many years before the eventual passage of the 1986 immigration law (IRCA) similarly, and convincingly, made the provisions salient to all Latinos (as seen, for example, in the 1984 data on the support of all Mexican Americans for amnesty) and coincided with a period in which Latino electoral participation in the United States increased substantially.

Whatever impact the current debate over immigration has on issue preferences, it is already affecting naturalization. Citizenship applications are up nationwide, and dramatically in California. The potential effect on the weight of Latinos among voters is large. As of 1990, there were 21.9 million Latinos in the United States; of these, 5.8 million, or over one-quarter of the total, were noncitizens (U.S. Bureau of the Census 1993). Moreover, 84 percent of the noncitizens are of voting age versus just over half (53 percent) of U.S.–born Latinos[29] (U.S. Bureau of the Census 1993). Thus, were all adult Latino noncitizens to naturalize, they would make up one-third of the Latino voting-age population and substantially increase the Latino proportion of the eligible electorate.[30]

This discussion has come full circle. The large number of Latinos, especially Mexican Americans, in California guarantees a significant role in state politics. The large number of noncitizen immigrants in the population, however, limits the amount of political influence. Policies targeting immigrants face overwhelming opposition from noncitizens and split the community of Mexican American citizens. However, these very policies are proving one of the most effective spurs yet to increasing the number of citizens and thereby, in the not very long run, enhancing Latino political power.

References

Cain, Bruce E., D. Roderick Kiewiet, and Carole J. Uhlaner. 1991. "The Acquisition of Partisanship by Latinos and Asian Americans," *American Journal of Political Science* 35 (May): 390–422.

Conway, M. Margaret. 1991. *Political Participation in the United States.* 2d ed. Washington, D.C.: CQ Press.

---

[29] Ninety-three percent of the 2.1 million naturalized immigrants are voting age (U.S. Bureau of the Census 1993).

[30] Of course, some noncitizens are not eligible for citizenship, either because they are not documented or because they have not yet met the residency requirement. The point of this calculation is to dramatically illustrate the magnitude of the importance of naturalization in increasing potential voting strength.

de la Garza, Rodolfo O., Louis DeSipio, F. Chris García, John García, and Angelo Falcón. 1992. *Latino Voices: Mexican, Puerto Rican, and Cuban Perspectives on American Politics*. Boulder, Colo.: Westview.

DeSipio, Louis. 1996. "Making Citizens or Good Citizens? Naturalization as a Predictor of Organizational and Electoral Behavior among Latino Immigrants," *Hispanic Journal of Behavioral Sciences* 18 (May): 194–213.

Field Institute. 1994. *Field (California) Poll, October, 1994*. [machine-readable data file]. San Francisco, Calif.: The Institute, Field (California) Poll 94-07.

———. 1995. "Voting in the 1994 General Election," *California Opinion Index*, January.

McDonnell, Patrick J. 1995. "Applications for Citizenship Soar in L.A.," *Los Angeles Times*, April 10.

Miller, Arthur H., Patricia Gurin, Gerald Gurin, and Oksana Malanchuk. 1981. "Group Consciousness and Political Participation," *American Journal of Political Science* 25 (August): 494–511.

NALEO Educational Fund. 1992. "Who Are Our Newest Latino U.S. Citizens?" *NLIS Research Notes* 1 (9): 1–4.

Southwest Voter Research Institute. 1995. "Record California Latino Vote Returns Feinstein to Senate," *Southwest Voter Research Notes* 9 (1): 1, 3.

Tomás Rivera Center. 1996. *The Latino Vote at Mid-Decade*. Claremont, Calif.: The Center.

Uhlaner, Carole Jean. 1989a. "'Relational Goods' and Participation: Incorporating Sociability into a Theory of Rational Action," *Public Choice* 62: 253–85.

———. 1989b. "Rational Turnout: The Neglected Role of Groups," *American Journal of Political Science* 33 (May): 390–422.

———. 1991a. "Political Participation and Discrimination: A Comparative Analysis of Asians, Blacks, and Latinos." In *Political Participation and American Democracy*, edited by William Crotty. New York: Greenwood.

———. 1991b. "Perceived Discrimination and Prejudice and the Coalition Prospects of Blacks, Latinos, and Asian Americans." In *Racial and Ethnic Politics in California*, edited by Byran O. Jackson and Michael B. Preston. Berkeley, Calif.: IGS Press.

———. n.d. "Political Action and Preferences of African-Americans, Latinos, and Asian Americans: Turning Numbers into Influence." In *Immigration and Race Relations*, edited by Gerald D. Jaynes. New Haven, Conn.: Yale University Press, forthcoming 1996.

Uhlaner, Carole Jean, Bruce E. Cain, and D. Roderick Kiewiet. 1989. "Political Participation of Ethnic Minorities in the 1980s," *Political Behavior* 11 (3): 195–231.

U. S. Bureau of the Census. 1989. *The Hispanic Population in the United States: March 1988*. Current Population Reports, Series P-20, No. 438. Washington, D.C.: U.S. Government Printing Office.

———. 1991. *Statistical Abstract of the United States: 1991*. Washington, D. C.: U.S. Government Printing Office.

———. 1993. *1990 Census of Population: Persons of Hispanic Origin in the United States*. 1990 CP-3-3, by Susan Lapham. Washington, D.C.: U.S. Government Printing Office.

Verba, Sidney, and Norman H. Nie. 1972. *Participation in America: Political Democracy and Social Equality*. New York: Harper and Row.

Verba, Sidney, Norman H. Nie, and Jae-on Kim. 1978. *Participation and Political Equality: A Seven-Nation Comparison*. Cambridge: Cambridge University Press.

Verba, Sidney, Kay Lehman Schlozman, Henry Brady, and Norman H. Nie. 1993. "Race, Ethnicity and Political Resources: Participation in the United States," *British Journal of Political Science* 23: 453–97.

Verhovek, Sam Howe. 1995. "Legal Immigrants Seek Citizenship in Record Numbers," *New York Times*, April 2.

4

Demographic Limitations to Latino Political Potential in San Diego

Leo F. Estrada

Introduction

The growth of the Latino population was one of the most dramatic demographic phenomena observed in the United States during the 1980s and early 1990s. Throughout these years the general national population was characterized by declining fertility due to later marriages, postponements of births, and high proportions of never-married women in peak childbearing years. The growth observed for Latinos in all parts of the United States during this same period is at a crosscurrent to these general trends. San Diego County, in Southern California, serves as a microcosm in which to examine the dominant patterns prevailing among the Latino population and the implications they might have for Latinos' political potential.

San Diego County's Latino population, as well as its Asian population, has consistently demonstrated dramatic growth rates. This growth is especially noteworthy given that it has occurred in a context (Southern California) in which growth is the norm (table 4.1): Latinos increased their numbers at a rate four times that of Anglos and twice that of African Americans. In 1990, there were a half-million Latinos in San Diego County; one of every five country residents was a Latino.

Assuming that the current growth rates for Latinos in San Diego continue into the future, projections point to an increase from 515,400 in 1994 to 763,400 in the year 2,000; 1 million in 2010; 1.3 million by 2020; 1.7 million by 2030; and 2.1 million in 2040. By 2040, Latinos are expected to comprise 76 percent of San Diego County's population.

Latino growth is not difficult to explain. Latinos are a youthful population, with a high proportion of women in their childbearing years. Latinos are also characterized by higher fertility and lower mortality rates, as well as by a large net flow of immigrants from Spanish-origin countries. For these reasons, it is clear that Latino growth will continue well into the new century.

TABLE 4.1
POPULATION GROWTH IN SAN DIEGO COUNTY, 1980–1990

Group	1980	1990	Difference	% Growth
Anglos				
N	1,371,807	1,639,845	268,038	19.54
% of Total	73.68	65.64		
Latinos				
N	274,530	498,578	224,048	81.61
% of Total	14.74	19.96		
African Americans				
N	104,407	150,670	46,263	44.31
% of Total	5.61	6.03		
Asians				
N	95,090	188,087	92,997	97.80
% of Total	5.11	7.53		

Limitations to Political Participation

Geographic Concentration

Regardless of their notable growth, Latinos still comprise only 20 percent of the population in San Diego County. Such a figure is not overly impressive from a political viewpoint because it is not the overall proportion, but rather the geographic concentration, of Latino growth that holds the potential for important political power.

In most cities of the Southwestern United States, Latinos tend to be less residentially segregated than other groups. San Diego is no exception. For example, Latinos are far less likely than African Americans to be concentrated in the inner city; this pattern is reinforced by the fact that the immense size of the county's geographic area results in a very high proportion of "suburbanites," regardless of race and ethnicity. The lack of residential concentration presents a disadvantage for Latinos, since geographically concentrated areas provide opportunities to exercise electoral power. Redistricting efforts, for example, attempt to concentrate ethnic populations into effective voting districts. These efforts are made more difficult and complex when there is no geographic concentration.

Given the growth of the Latino population in San Diego and its lack of geographic concentration, one might expect that Latinos are a "swing vote" in close elections. Some might argue that this explains why the number of Latino elected officials lags far behind the population's growth. While lack of geographic concentration is a factor, there are other equally significant demographic constraints on Latinos' political participation in San Diego and, by extension, further afield.

Too Young to Vote: Age Constraints

The youthfulness of this population is largely responsible for the higher number of births observed for Latinos in San Diego. The median age for Latinos in San Diego is 24.4 years, compared to 25.2 years for African Americans and 34.3 years for Anglos. It is estimated that by the year 2000, Latino median age will reach 28.3, compared to 39.3 for Anglos, maintaining the decade-long gap between Latinos and Anglos. These differences in age structure account for the larger proportion of Latinas of childbearing age, particularly in the peak childbearing years between the ages of nineteen and twenty-nine.

According to the 1994 Current Population Survey (CPS), the number of Latinos in California exceeds ten million, and they represent about 31 percent of the state's population. Almost 40 percent of Latinos are under the age of eighteen. Adults comprise 57 percent of the Latino population, but Latino elderly are only 4 percent of the total in this population.

Youthful populations are of great interest to demographic analysts who seek to project future populations. But to political analysts, youthful populations represent ineligible voters, at least in the short run. In San Diego County, over one-third of all Latinos are under seventeen years of age and thus too young to participate in the electoral process (table 4.2). Table 4.3 confirms the difference between Latinos and Anglos in terms of their adult populations. Eight of every ten Anglos fall into the adult category, but only six of every ten Latinos are adults.

While youthfulness reduces the influence that a population can have in an election today, youthfulness also represents a pool of potential voters who will come of electoral age in the upcoming years. In fact, the number of Latino youths in San Diego County who have joined the voting-age population each year since 1990 is substantial. And by 1998, at least 70,000 Latinos will move into the adult voting-age population. By 2003, that number will rise to over 120,000. Of course, some of these teens will move to other areas before they reach age eighteen, but their numbers will be offset by the flows of citizen children of Latino families that move into San Diego County.

TABLE 4.2
AGE DISTRIBUTION IN CALIFORNIA BY RACE AND ETHNICITY, 1994
(PERCENTAGES)

Group	0–17 Yrs.	18–64 Yrs.	65+ Yrs.
Anglos	48	58	78
Latinos	35	25	10
African Americans	8	7	5
Asians/Other	11	10	7

Source: Current Population Survey, November 1994.

TABLE 4.3
VOTING-AGE POPULATION IN SELECTED METROPOLITAN AREAS

Metropolitan Area	% Over Age 18	% of Anglos Over Age 18	% of Latinos Over Age 18
Los Angeles	67.6	80.9	64.8
San Diego	75.5	79.9	64.8
Fresno	71.0	80.9	60.7

Source: Current Population Survey, March 1995. Based on adults aged 18 and over living in telephone households.

Ineligible Populations: Noncitizen Constraints

While in large part the growth of the Latino population is due to natural increase (births minus deaths), immigration, both legal and unauthorized, is also a strong contributing factor to Latino growth rates. Among Latino adults in California, 38 percent are U.S. born, 8 percent are naturalized citizens, and 54 percent are not citizens—that is, immigrants. By contrast, among all Latino children in California in 1994, 84 percent are U.S. born, compared to 16 percent born abroad.

Table 4.4 shows that San Diego is a major port of entry for immigrants from Spanish-origin and Pacific Rim countries. While Asian populations show the highest proportion of foreign born, their lower proportion of noncitizens indicates that they are naturalizing at a rapid pace. Since many Asians, particularly Southeast Asians, entered the United States as refugees, they have ready access to government-sponsored language training and citizenship classes not available to non-refugee groups.

TABLE 4.4
FOREIGN-BORN POPULATION OF SAN DIEGO COUNTY, 1990

Status	Latinos	Anglos	African Americans	Asians
U.S.–born	285,188	1,550,925	150,706	74,545
% U.S.–born	57.2	94.6	95.7	37.5
Foreign-born	213,390	88,920	6,789	124,130
Noncitizen	166,980	39,747	4,414	65,045
% Noncitizen	78.2	44.70	65.0	52.4

Ineligibility due to foreign birth is only a temporary problem if a non–U.S.-born person enters legally, resides continually in the United States for at least five years, applies with the Immigration and Naturalization Service for a change in status, and moves through the naturalization procedure. This process has been followed by previous European immigrant groups, as well as more recently by Asians and Cuban-born Latinos. However, Mexico-born foreign persons, who comprise the largest foreign-born group in the United States, are typically hesitant to naturalize.

To a great extent, nonparticipation in the political arena can be attributed to this lower rate of naturalization for Mexican-origin legal residents. Voting data from the Current Population Survey reflect that 84 percent of nonvoting Latino adults indicated noncitizen status (ineligibility) as the primary reason for not voting. In 1980, only 16 percent of Mexico-born residents had opted to become naturalized citizens. More recent studies place this figure at 22 percent. While this gain is important, the naturalization rate for Latinos still lags far behind levels of over 50 percent for Vietnamese and Filipinos.

Ironically, voting studies have generally found that nonvoting Mexican immigrants nevertheless assign very positive values to voting. Nevertheless, although Mexican immigrants are favorably inclined toward voting, the process of naturalization operates as a barrier to their exercise of that vote.

Table 4.5, based on CPS voting data, indicates that the weight of ineligibility due to noncitizenship falls most heavily on the Latino population. Although Latinos represent about 11 percent of the national population, their adult foreign-born population accounts for 36 percent of all adult noncitizens.

TABLE 4.5

CITIZENS AND NONVOTING ELIGIBLE ADULTS IN UNITED STATES, 1994
(1000s)

	All Persons	Citizens	Noncitizens	Citizenship
Anglos	160,317	150,287	10,030	93.7
Latinos	17,476	9,813	7,663	56.2
African Americans	21,799	20,718	1,081	95.0
Asians	4,849	2,183	2,666	45.0

Source: Current Population Survey, November 1994.

The vast majority of immigrants arrive in the United States during their early working years (eligible voting ages). It is estimated that more than two million Mexican immigrants are legally present in the United States and could currently be naturalized. This number would be in addition to the one million Latinos who applied for permanent resident status under the 1986 Immigration Reform and Control Act (IRCA) and are currently in the "pipeline" toward citizenship.

Citizenship campaigns are a good investment, since the voting rate for naturalized citizens has been found to be slightly higher than that for U.S.–born citizens (61 percent versus 55 percent, respectively). Thus the naturalization efforts linked to voter registration drives are capable of quickly raising the number of eligible Latino voters and the overall Latino voter turnout rate.

Voter Registration and Turnout

Voter registration has increased among Latinos in recent decades. The 1994 Current Population Survey estimated that there are 5.2 million Latino registered voters nationally, and over one million new Latino registered voters have been added to the voting rolls since 1984. This increase in voter registration is due in part to overall population growth, increases in the rate of Latino registration, and particularly high increments in the forty-five to sixty-four age group. Nonetheless, despite these gains, CPS data indicate that only 26 percent of all voting-age Latino adults are registered voters.

While voter registration is lower for Latinos than for other groups, these rates are exaggerated relative to other groups because they are calculated using the adult population (eighteen years of age and older) as the denominator. When the calculations are based on the *eligible* adult population as the denominator—that is, excluding noncitizens—the voter registration rates for Latinos, while still the lowest, rise to about 56 percent. Seen in this manner, among eligible Hispanic adults, a bit more than half register to vote.

According to the CPS data, approximately ten million eligible adult Latino citizens in the United States are not registered to vote. In addition, there is a latent pool of one million Latino legal residents who could begin the naturalization process immediately if they chose to do so.

On a positive note, among those Latinos who are registered, the turnout rate is high and approximates the rates of other groups (table 4.6). While turnout fluctuates greatly from one election to the next, the gap between Anglo turnout and Latino turnout is closing.

TABLE 4.6
VOTING AND REGISTRATION IN THE UNITED STATES,
BY RACE AND ETHNICITY

	Registered as % of Total Voting-age Population	Voters as % of Voting-age Population	Voters as % of Registered Voting-age Population
Anglos	77	68	90
Latinos	26	20	88
African Americans	78	65	86
Asians/ Other	39	33	86

Source: Current Population Survey, 1994.

Factors Related to Voting Behavior

Researchers have identified several factors that are associated with
voter registration and turnout. Most of the factors related to enhancing voter participation run in somewhat opposite direction to the
characteristics typically found in the Latino population.

AGE

Voting has been found to be related to age: the older a person, the
more likely he or she is to register and vote. Only 20 percent of eight-
een- to twenty-four-year-olds vote, compared to 61 percent of the elderly (table 4.7). As indicated earlier, Latinos in general, including in
San Diego, are youthful and thus more likely to have the lowest voting rate.

TABLE 4.7
PARTICIPATING VOTERS IN THE UNITED STATES, BY AGE,
NOVEMBER 1994 (1000S)

Age	All Persons	Citizens	% Voting, All Persons	% Voting, All Citizens
18–24	25,182	22,675	20.0	22.2
25–44	83,006	75,296	39.1	43.1
45–64	50,934	47,643	56.0	59.9
65+	31,144	29,833	60.7	63.3

EDUCATION

Voting is also associated with higher levels of education. Table 4.8
confirms that pattern, with one-quarter of those with less than an
eighth-grade education voting, compared to two-thirds of those with
a college or advanced degree.

Unfortunately, educational attainment is relatively low for Latinos. In San Diego County, among Latino adults aged twenty-five and
older, 13 percent had less than a fifth-grade education, 28 percent had
less than a ninth-grade education, 19 percent had a high school degree, and only 9 percent had a college or advanced degree. Low educational attainment is a characteristic that distinguishes Latinos from
other groups in California. Educational attainment among Latino

adults is dismally low, lagging behind Anglos by four years of education and behind African Americans by three years. Overall, Latino adults are the group least likely to have graduated from high school.

TABLE 4.8
EDUCATIONAL ACHIEVEMENT AND VOTING IN THE UNITED STATES,
NOVEMBER 1994 (1000s)

Years of Education	N	% Registered	% Voted
0–8	14,734	40.1	23.2
9–11	20,717	44.7	27.0
12	64,929	58.9	40.5
1–3 of College	50,441	68.4	49.1
College Degree	39,446	76.3	63.1

On a positive note, educational progress can be observed since 1990, particularly across immigrant generations. The educational attainment of both parents and their children improves over time in the United States (table 4.9). Within California's current Latino population, 62 percent of Latino adults are first generation, 29 percent are second generation, and 19 percent are third generation. However, for children under the age of seventeen (the next generation of adults), that distribution shifts noticeably—16 percent are first generation, 60 percent are second generation, and 24 percent are third generation or more. These figures portend improving education levels as these younger age cohorts enter adulthood.

TABLE 4.9
EDUCATIONAL ACHIEVEMENT (YEARS OF SCHOOLING)
BY IMMIGRANT GENERATION

	First Generation	Second Generation	Third Generation
Respondent	8.8	10.9	11.9
Father	5.0	6.5	8.2
Mother	4.1	6.0	8.9

Note: First generation are persons born abroad; second generation are persons born of foreign-born parents; third generation are persons born in the United States of U.S.–born parents.

LABOR FORCE PARTICIPATION AND OCCUPATION

Voting behavior is also linked with employment and active participation in the labor force. Only 28 percent of the unemployed vote, compared to 45 percent of the employed (table 4.10). On this factor, Latinos are aligned with higher propensities for voting; the differences in labor force participation among Anglos and Latinos in San Diego County are small (table 4.11), a fact that should bolster Latino participation. However, among the employed, voting behavior is strongest among those in higher-skilled occupations. Table 4.12 compares the occupational distribution of Anglos and Latinos in San Diego. These data demonstrate that Latino males typically cluster in service or blue-collar, craftsman, and operator occupations. In contrast, Anglo males are more likely to have technical, managerial, and sales occupations.

TABLE 4.10
VOTING AND LABOR FORCE STATUS IN THE UNITED STATES
(1000s)

Employment Status	All Persons	Citizens	% Voting, All Persons	% Voting, All Citizens
Employed	122,584	113,596	45.2	48.8
Unemployed	6,492	5,705	28.3	32.2
Not in Labor Force	61,191	56,147	45.3	49.4

Source: Current Population Survey, November 1994.

TABLE 4.11
LABOR FORCE PARTICIPATION IN CALIFORNIA AND SAN DIEGO COUNTY,
BY RACE AND ETHNICITY (PERCENTAGES)

Labor Force Participation	California	San Diego
Anglos	75	67.9
Latinos	80	68.6
African Americans	65	71.9
Asians/Other	68	68.9

Lack of employment is inversely associated with voting behavior, with currently employed workers more likely to vote. In regard to this factor, unemployment rates are higher for Latinos than for Anglos, and the difference is stronger in San Diego than in California as a whole. In 1990, 11 percent of California's Latinos were unemployed, compared to 8 percent among the Anglo population. In that same year, Anglo unemployment in San Diego measured 4.7 percent, while the corresponding figure for Latinos was 9.5 percent.

TABLE 4.12
OCCUPATION LEVELS FOR LATINO AND ANGLO MALES IN
SAN DIEGO COUNTY, 1990 (PERCENTAGES)

Occupational Level	Latinos	Anglos
Managerial/ Professional	14.7	35.1
Technical/Sales	25.5	35.0
Services	22.5	10.5
Crafts	13.3	10.6
Operator	17.2	7.7
Farmwork	6.8	1.1

FAMILY INCOME

Higher levels of educational attainment lead to higher-level occupations, where employment is more secure and better remunerated. The percentages for both registration and voting in the 1994 election increase with higher family income levels (table 4.13). For example, only one of five persons earning less than $5,000 a year votes, compared to three of every five persons earning over $50,000. Despite the growth of family income since 1980, Latinos and African Americans lag behind Asians and Anglos in median family income (table 4.14).

These income figures are more dramatic when one considers the number of family members who share that income. Because Latino families tend to be large (4.1 members on average in San Diego in 1995, compared to 2.5 in Anglo families, 3.0 for African Americans, and 3.5 for Asians), per capita income in Latino families is exceedingly low.

TABLE 4.13
FAMILY INCOME AND VOTING, NOVEMBER 1994

Income	N (1000s)	% Registered to Vote	% Voted
Under $5,000	4,510	40.4	19.9
$5,000–9,999	8,086	42.9	23.3
$10,000–14,999	11,477	51.7	32.7
$15,000–24,999	20,267	57.4	39.9
$25,000–34,999	21,837	62.5	44.4
$35,000–49,999	25,902	67.7	49.8
$50,000 +	44,530	76.2	60.1

TABLE 4.14
MEDIAN FAMILY INCOME IN SAN DIEGO COUNTY,
BY RACE AND ETHNICITY

Group	1980	1990
Anglos	$23,882	$44,289
Latinos	$17,727	$26,453
African Americans	$16,070	$26,768
Asians/Other	$23,907	$38,369

Source: U.S. Census, 1980 and 1990.

HOMEOWNERSHIP

A final factor that has been found to be associated with voting is homeownership. Seventy percent of homeowners report that they voted, compared to 43 percent of renters. In San Diego, there is a marked difference in homeownership between Anglos and Asians, on the one hand, and Latinos and African Americans, on the other: the majority of Asians and Anglos own their homes, while the majority of Latinos and African Americans rent (table 4.15).

TABLE 4.15
HOUSING TENURE IN SAN DIEGO COUNTY,
BY RACE AND ETHNICITY, 1990

Group	Percent That Rents	Percent That Owns
Anglos	35	65
Latinos	62	38
African Americans	64	36
Asians	49	51
Other	40	60
Average	45	55

Latino Voting Potential

Although one of every three persons in California is a Latino, Latinos account for but one of every ten voters in California. Thus, although the power of the Latino vote in California is not insignificant, it is far from overwhelming. For the time being, Latino voting power will prove most important at the local level, where the size and geographic concentration of the Latino population provide the electoral potential to swing a close election.

These results are not surprising. A high proportion of Latinos are too young to vote. An equally high proportion of Latinos are ineligible to vote. And, with the exception of labor force participation, on all the other demographic factors associated with voting, Latinos are either on the lowest rung or are clearly lagging behind other groups.

Under the circumstances, although Latino populations are numerous and growing, every one hundred Latino residents produce only about fourteen votes, compared to forty-nine votes derived from every one hundred Anglo residents (see table 4.16). The implications of these figures are clear. To create a district where one could be reasonably assured that Latinos would be able to dominate the electorate, Latinos would have to comprise at least 75 percent of all residents. This is an exceedingly high proportion to attain for large electoral districts, particularly if the population in question is not "hyper-segregated."

TABLE 4.16
"TYPICAL" VOTING SCENARIO FOR "REPRESENTATIVE"
ANGLO AND LATINO POPULATIONS

	"Typical" Anglo Population	"Typical" Latino Population
Representative Population	100	100
N Too Young to Vote	-21	-36
Voting-age Population	79	64
Ineligible to Vote	-4	-34
Citizen Voting-age Population	75	30
Nonregistered Voters	-21	-15
Registered Voters	54	15
Voters in an Election	49	14

Conclusions

From the foregoing discussion, one might surmise that Latinos in San Diego, and in California more generally, would have difficulty playing a significant role in the electoral process. Actually the opposite is the case. Latinos have held a seat on the San Diego City Council for the past decade, ever since the single-member redistricting plan was challenged and modified in the late 1980s. Denise Moreno Ducheny holds the 79th seat in the California State Assembly. And recently City Council Member Juan Vargas challenged an incumbent for the 50th congressional seat. In the past, the 40th Senate seat has been occupied by a Latino, and it is not unlikely that a Latino might retake that seat in the near future.

Thus, despite the absence of high-propensity voting characteristics in the Latino population, there is a demonstrated ability to elect Latinos in local elections. This can be credited to the ability of Latino candidates to bridge to, and garner the votes of, non-Latino groups. In the recent 1996 primary elections, Assemblywoman Ducheny received half of the Democratic vote, possible only by attracting a considerable number of Anglo and Asian voters. Likewise, Councilman Vargas obtained about 15,000 votes, sufficient to come in a close second in a multi-candidate race, demonstrating that he, too, had sufficient appeal to non-Latinos to make his candidacy a viable one.

The lesson to be learned here is that Latinos, despite their phenomenal growth, do not have within their own ranks sufficient voters to elect Latino candidates. Thus Latino office seekers in San Diego have, by necessity, learned the art of cross-ethnic appeal, campaigning, and representation—a valuable lesson for all of California.

Likewise, due to their large numbers but few voters, Latinos in San Diego, and California in general, must learn to mobilize and flex their "constituency power." For whether they vote or not, Latino constituents (in collectives) can hold their elected representatives accountable and demand attention to their particular communities' needs.

5

The Challenge of Latino Education: Implications for Social and Educational Policy

Patricia Gándara

The National Context

The challenge of Latino education is often described as a "pipeline" problem—that is, a failure to keep Latino students in the educational pipeline leading to high school graduation and postsecondary education. The statistic of a 50 percent dropout rate for Latino students in some urban high schools is now well known (Fernández and Shu 1988), but the leaky pipeline problem begins long before students show up as dropout statistics. Latino children are born into poverty at much higher rates than Anglo children: 39 percent of Latino children were born into families living below the poverty line in 1992, compared to 16 percent of non-Hispanic white children (NCES 1995a). This devastatingly high percentage of Latino children living in poverty sets the stage for future difficulties in education. At ages three and four, just 17 percent of Latino children are in preschool programs (largely Head Start and other government-sponsored programs) that prepare children for school entry. Meanwhile, 38 percent of non-Hispanic white children are enrolled in preschools, most of which are privately operated and offer a wider range of approaches and greater exposure to middle-class children and families. Moreover, while preschool attendance rates have been increasing steadily for Anglo children, Latino preschool attendance in 1993 was approximately the same as twenty years earlier (NCES 1995a), reflecting the relatively steady funding for poor children's services (Phillips 1990). Hence, before the children even begin their formal education, Latino students are already at a serious disadvantage.

By age nine, significant gaps between Latino and non-Latino white students have emerged in all subjects, and by age thirteen Latinos are approximately two years behind Anglo students in both reading and math and four years behind in science. These gaps persist over time, so that by age seventeen, Latino students' reading and science ability is approximately the same as that of thirteen-year-old Anglo students (NCES 1995a). Moreover, because dropout rates are so high for Latino students, those included in these comparisons represent only the students who have elected to stay in school—between 60 and 70 percent of all Latino seventeen-year-olds, compared with approximately 90 percent of non-Hispanic white seventeen-year-olds. Consistent with these statistics, Latino high school students are significantly less likely than non-Hispanic white students to take advanced math (geometry, algebra II, trigonometry, and calculus) and advanced science (chemistry and physics) courses which would prepare them for postsecondary education (see table 5.1).

TABLE 5.1
PERCENTAGE OF HIGH SCHOOL STUDENTS TAKING SELECTED COURSES
(1992)

Math & Science Courses	Anglo	Hispanic
Remedial Math	14.6	24.2
Algebra I	94.0	92.5
Geometry	72.6	62.9
Algebra II	59.2	46.9
Trigonometry	22.5	15.2
Calculus	10.7	4.7
Biology	93.5	91.2
Chemistry	58.0	42.6
Physics	25.9	15.7
Biology, Chemistry, and Physics	22.6	12.8

Sources: NCES, High School and Beyond Transcript Study and National Education Longitudinal Study Transcripts, 1992.

Hence, at the point of matriculating from high school, Latino students lag far behind Anglo students on every dimension. While approximately 12 percent of the college-age population is Latino, less than 5 percent of four-year college students are Latino (NCES 1995b). Many fewer Latino students than non-Hispanic whites complete a college degree: in the 25–29 age group, only 13 percent of Latinos had completed a bachelor's degree, while 30 percent of Anglo students had. And among those who complete bachelor's degrees, Latino students take substantially longer to achieve this goal (see table 5.2).

TABLE 5.2
YEARS TO COMPLETE BA FOR LATINO AND ANGLO STUDENTS
(PERCENTAGES)

Race/Ethnicity	4 or less	5 or less	6 or less	More than 6
Anglo	44.4	71.6	81.5	18.5
Hispanic	31.1	60.3	72.9	27.1

Source: NCES, recent college graduate surveys.

The California Context

While the Latino population nationwide is heterogeneous and comprises significant portions of Mexican Americans, Puerto Ricans, Cubans, Central Americans, and others, the Latino population of California is much less varied. Up to 85 percent of California Latinos are of Mexican descent (LES 1993a), and this group has been cited as the most educationally "at risk" of all Latino subgroups (De la Rosa and Maw 1990; Aguirre and Martínez 1993), largely because they have the lowest rates of school persistence (see table 5.3). Hence the challenge of Latino education nationwide is far more acute in California and other parts of the Southwest where Mexican Americans predominate.

In the upcoming 1996–97 school year, the population trend lines will cross over and Latinos will become the most numerous students in California schools; while Anglo students will comprise barely 39 percent of the school population, Latinos will exceed 40 percent. By the year 2004, the California Department of Finance estimates that

Latinos will comprise more than 50 percent of the public school population (California Department of Finance 1996).[1]

TABLE 5.3
SCHOOLING COMPLETED BY RACE/ETHNICITY FOR
PERSONS AGED 25 YEARS AND OLDER
(PERCENTAGES)

Race/ Ethnicity	% Completing 4 Yrs or More of High School		% Completing 4 Yrs or More of College	
	1980	1990	1980	1990
Asian	74..5	80.4	32.9	39.9
Anglo	69.6	79.1	17.4	28.5
African American	51.2	65.5	8.5	11.4
Puerto Rican	45.9	55.5	5.6	9.7
Cuban	44.6	63.5	12.1	20.2
Chicano	38.1	44.1	4.9	5.4

Source: A. Aguirre and R. Martínez, *Chicanos in Higher Education* (Washington, D.C.: George Washington University, 1993).

The pipeline problem in California is best exemplified by the fact that of every one hundred Latino students in tenth grade, only four will become eligible to attend the University of California upon graduation, and only one will actually enroll, although the top 12.5 percent of the state's students will be eligible to attend, according to unpublished data from the Office of the President of the University of California. Even if Latinos represented a smaller portion of California's population, this would present a serious problem; but in light of their large numbers, it is nothing short of a crisis. While there has been some slow progress in Latino college eligibility rates, the Latino Eligibility Study estimates that, at the current rate, it would take forty-three years for Latinos to become eligible for university atten-

---

[1]Ironically, while the student population of the state continues to diversify, particularly with respect to Latino representation, the teacher population has remained stable over the last decade, with approximately 80 percent of the state's teachers being nonminority white and approximately 9 percent Latino (PACE 1995).

dance in numbers proportionate to their representation in the population (LES 1993a). Table 5.4 demonstrates the substantial discrepancy between university enrollments and representation in the population for Latinos in California.

TABLE 5.4
1992–93 UNIVERSITY OF CALIFORNIA ENROLLMENTS
AS PERCENTAGE OF COHORT

Program	Total Students	Latinos	% Latinos	Latinos as % of Age Cohort
Senior				
Class	30,767	3,135	10	34
Master's	8,702	615	7	34
Ph.D.	4,926	220	4	34
Law	2,167	235	11	34
Medicine	6,855	438	6	34

Issues of gender are also pertinent to the discussion of the educational pipeline. Although their numbers remain small, Latinas (and Chicanas, to a lesser extent) have made significant strides in education in recent times. Between 1983 and 1993, the Latina population in California increased by more than 50 percent; meanwhile their participation in undergraduate education within the University of California system increased by 250 percent, from 471 women in the senior class of 1983 to 1,662 women in the 1993 senior class. Moreover, they appear to be persisting at the same rate as Latino males: Latinas were 53 percent of all Hispanics in the freshman class in 1989, and they remained 53 percent of the Hispanics in their senior class in 1992–93. Because there are fewer females than males in this age group, the actual discrepancy between male and female Latinos is about 10 percentage points in favor of the women. Compared to Latino males, Latinas have made large strides in undergraduate participation within the university.

However, while Latinas have increased substantially their participation in undergraduate education at the University of California over the last decade and have been closing the gap between themselves and their male counterparts, these gains do not come near to closing the gap between themselves and all women, nor between themselves and male Latinos at the graduate education level. As seen in table 5.5, while Latinos comprised about 23 percent of the college-

TABLE 5.5
UNIVERSITY OF CALIFORNIA ENROLLMENT, 1983 AND 1992–93

1983	No. of Men	No. of Women	Women as % of Total	No. of Latinas	Latinas as % of Total	Latinas as % of All Women	Latinas as % of All Latinos	Latinos as % of Age Group
Sr. Class	10,569	9,373	47	471	2.3	4.0	44	
Master's	5,694	5,471	49	221	1.9	4.2	52	
Ph.D.	2,422	1,248	34	52	1.4	5.0	43	23
Law	1,302	943	42	98	4.4	10.0	42	
Medicine	2,892	1,773	38	133	2.9	7.5	30	

1992–93	No. of Men	No. of Women	Women as % of Total	No. of Latinas	Latinas as % of Total	Latinas as % of All Women	Latinas as % of all Latinos	Latinos as % of Age Group
Sr. Class	15,691	15,076	49	1,662	5.4	11.0	53	
Master's	3,916	4,786	55	320	3.7	6.6	52	
Ph.D.	3,005	1,921	39	90	1.8	4.6	41	34
Law	1,235	932	43	106	4.9	11.0	45	
Medicine	4,570	2,285	50	175	3.8	7.6	40	

Source: California Postsecondary Education Commission, 1993.

age population in 1983, Latinas accounted for only 4 percent of all of the women in the University of California's senior class. By 1992–93, they were 11 percent of the women in the senior class, but Latinos constituted 34 percent of the population in this age group. Hence their representation is growing, but there is a long way to go before reaching overall parity.

At the level of doctoral education, 39 percent of all Ph.D. students in 1992–93 were women, but only 4.6 percent of all women Ph.D. students were Latinas. Moreover, while women as a whole made a 5-percentage-point gain in their share among Ph.D. students (from 34 to 39 percent) between 1983 and 1992, Latinas lost 2 percentage points (from 43 to 41) as a proportion of all Hispanic doctoral students, as well as dropping from 5 percent to 4.6 percent of all women pursuing Ph.D.s.

Hence, while women have made substantial progress over the 1983–1993 period, meeting or approaching gender parity in all areas except Ph.D.–level studies, Latinas have a much longer road to travel. They represent roughly 15 percent of the college-age population, but in every case except the undergraduate level they fail to reach even the 5 percent mark in university participation. They are fewer than 2 percent of all Ph.D. students in the state, and at the doctoral and professional level Latinas have yet to achieve parity with Latino males.

The issue of graduate education becomes especially important in light of the fact that graduate students form the next generation of professionals—individuals who have a significant and direct impact on social policy. While it is critically important to bring more Latino students through the pipeline to high school and college graduation so that they may be prepared for the job market and for meaningful participation in the body politic, it is equally important to nurture a new generation of managers and professionals if Latinos are ever to have a potent voice in shaping their own futures. Moreover, because Latino faculty often feel the greatest personal responsibility for mentoring Latino students, and because they model both the *desirability* and the *achievability* of becoming a faculty member, it is critical that Latinos have a presence among the professoriate. However, in a state in which Latinos make up almost a third of the population, only 4 percent of the faculty at the University of California are Latinos, and at the level of full professor only 3 percent are Latinos. Given the pace at which Latino faculty are hired and promoted, it would take well into the next millennium to achieve anything close to parity.

In sum, the pipeline of Latino students is leaking throughout the life cycle, from the earliest contact with education in homes that are disproportionately poor, through the school years, and into undergraduate and graduate education. At every point Latinos lose ground in comparison to other groups in society. Why is this? What accounts for this dismal picture?

Explaining Latino Underachievement

Many explanations have been offered for this state of affairs. Over time they have concentrated largely on the perceived deficits of the Latino population—in ability, achievement orientation, even linguistic capacity, in the sense that the frequency of reflexive verbs in the Spanish language presumably does not allow its speakers to take responsibility for their own actions (*se me hizo tarde* = I was made late)! Explanations for Latino school failure have shifted, roughly paralleling the decades since the 1960s when the problem first came to public notice.

In the 1960s, which saw the most impressive gains in U.S. history in terms of civil rights for minorities, the scholarly literature focused on *deprivation* theories and ways to ameliorate this disadvantage. Minorities, such as Mexican Americans, were viewed as having fundamental deficits which schools and government could overcome through special interventions such as Head Start (Hess and Shipman 1965; Valentine 1968). As these efforts appeared to meet with only limited success, and failed to change the fundamental relationships of students to schools, the focus shifted in the 1970s to a cultural difference model.

The *cultural difference* model suggested that Latinos were not so much "deprived" of important cultural experiences as they were participants in a different set of experiences which, while worthy in themselves, did not meet the expectations of schools (Carter and Segura 1979; Buenning and Tollefson 1987). One of the chief cultural differences between lower-income and middle-class students identified by researchers was speech style (Hymes 1974). This focus on speech and language differences was especially salient for Chicanos because of the obvious differences between the language of the home and the language of the school. Hence this discontinuity in linguistic experience, coupled with other cultural differences between home and school, came to explain academic failure.

The major educational response to this theory of failure was bilingual/bicultural education. In 1968, Title VII was enacted as an amendment to the Elementary and Secondary Education Act (ESEA) to address "the special educational needs of the large numbers of children of limited-English-speaking ability in the United States." Hence the 1970s opened with a new federal mandate to attempt to level the playing field for limited-English-proficient (LEP) (at that time, as now, largely Latino) children in the schools through bilingual education programs. Shortly thereafter, in 1976, California passed its Bilingual Education (Chacón-Moscone, 1976) bill and with it acknowledged the need to provide special services to these students. Nonetheless, no more than one-third of the limited-English students in California receive instruction from a bilingual teacher, and almost one-quarter of all California LEP students are not enrolled in any language assistance program (CDE 1996). Although bilingual education has often been characterized in the media as a failure, in reality it has never been made available to the vast majority of language-minority students in the state (Gándara 1986; Rumbaut and Cornelius 1995).

During this same period, a radical economic analysis of the plight of disenfranchised minorities gained currency. Its main exponents, Samuel Bowles and Herbert Gintis (1976), explained group differences in academic achievement as a function of capitalist economics. The economic determinism of Bowles and Gintis's work found a home among sociologists for whom *social reproduction* via the sorting of students according to social class in order to control the distribution of educational and economic opportunities resonated with particular fervor. This theory exposed the "hidden hand" of economic policy, yet it failed to explain differences among low-income and minority groups in their response to the American school system. In other words, it did not address the question of how some students manage to succeed in the system despite serious social and economic disadvantages.

As the 1970s' strong bias in favor of quantitative methods began to give way in the 1980s to qualitative methods drawn from anthropology, more powerful and complex explanatory theories of minority school failure emerged. This new literature, which focused on the *social construction of disadvantage*, had the benefit of being able to explain at least partially the differences *between* various immigrant and minority groups in their responses to education. Ogbu (1987; Ogbu and Matute-Bianchi 1986) articulated a framework for studying minority school achievement that distinguished between *immigrant minorities* (people who have come to the United States more or less voluntarily to seek greater opportunity) and *involuntary* or *caste-like minorities* (those individuals who find themselves in the United States through slavery, conquest, or colonization). According to this framework, immigrant minorities reference their situation in the United States to that in the homelands they fled. Despite the discrimination and other barriers facing newcomers, these minorities find their present situation to be a hopeful one. On the other hand, caste-like minorities mark as their reference point the members of their group who have already lived in the United States for generations and failed to secure a place within the mainstream. This results in an attitude of hopelessness and the adoption of behaviors defined in opposition to the practices and preferences of Anglo Americans. These adopted behaviors serve as a way of repudiating the negative stereotypes that the majority culture projects on them. If school achievement is a value of Anglo culture, doing well in school takes on the connotation of "acting white," anathema to the behavioral standards of the minority group. Ogbu and Matute-Bianchi applied the framework specifically to Mexican Americans to explain how group behaviors may result from, and reinforce, majority culture stereotypes that operate to maintain minority group subordination.

Mehan (1992) likewise argued that there exist structural impediments to minority achievement. He suggested that bureaucratic school organization operates to maintain status differences between majority- and minority-culture students through "constitutive rules," the rules of behavior and decision making that determine the kind of curriculum to which children will be exposed. Low-income and minority students, because they come to school without the status characteristics of the middle and upper classes, are assigned to the lower tracks and groups in school where they can be "remediated." Higher status students are placed in the upper tracks and the faster reading groups where they can fulfill the promise of their more monied and educated heritage. In this way, the structure of the school promotes the idea among low-income and minority students that they cannot, and should not, compete with their social and academic superiors. Thus Mehan viewed the school as a perhaps unintentional but nonetheless powerful co-conspirator in society's reproduction of class differences. To the extent that some immigrant and other low-income students mirror the achievement characteristics of the middle and upper classes—for example, adhering to the behavioral norms of the school, giving priority to studying over other kinds of activities—the *bureaucratic structure* of the schools can accommodate their mobility.

The *resistance* theorists offer a somewhat different explanation of minority school failure. Giroux (1983), Willis (1977), and MacLeod (1995) invoked the notion of social agency in their explanations of school failure. Within this framework, the student is no longer merely a pawn in an economic or bureaucratic structure but an active participant in deciding his or her own fate. Students' insights into their own circumstances, while often astute, can nonetheless be insufficient to allow them to break with their own cultural biases. Their resistance against what is perceived to be an unfair system may lead them to reject opportunities to "make it" within that system. The perspective of the resistance theorists shares much with the writing of Ogbu on oppositional features of minority culture, yet it differs in the extent to which the resistance theorists focus on individual, as opposed to group, agency—the capacity of the individual to interpret his or her own circumstances and respond accordingly. Mexican American students who "choose" to join gangs, drop out of school, and otherwise reject the social norms of Anglo society are a classic example of the enactment of oppositional behavior within the resistance theorists' framework. Such students cooperate in creating their own dismal situation as an act of defiance against a culture they perceive as oppressive.

A third contemporary perspective on school failure has its roots in the work of Bourdieu and Passeron (1977), but it has been applied to American youth in the work of Lareau (1987, 1989). From this perspective, variation in school achievement can be traced to differences in *cultural capital*, defined as the general cultural background, knowledge, disposition, and skills that are passed from one generation to another. Schools reward the cultural capital of the dominant classes (and, by association, that of the Anglo majority) and devalue that of the lower classes and ethnic minorities. Hence, as Lareau asserts in her study of working- and middle-class school communities, parents who understand and share the middle-class values of schools are able to intervene on their children's behalf to assure that they benefit from all the school has to offer. Lower-income and minority parents seldom share the same knowledge, disposition, and skills that would allow them to effect similar outcomes for their children.

More recently, Portes and Zhou (1993) suggested that *segmented assimilation* may account for the different adaptations of second-generation minority children to American society and schooling. Drawing from a large data set of children of immigrants on both U.S. coasts, as well as studies of Punjabi children in Northern California (Gibson 1988) and Mexican American and Japanese American children in California (Matute-Bianchi 1986), Portes and Zhou conclude that rapid assimilation into American culture can have disastrous consequences for the children of immigrant minorities.

Across the various immigrant groups, the most academically successful students were those who remained most closely allied with the culture of their parents. This seemingly paradoxical finding was explained in terms of group resources and attitudes. For Punjabi, Japanese, and Cuban American children, the fact that there are strong coethnic communities, with considerable social and economic resources, reinforces the respective parental culture. These children find it relatively easy to accommodate to the demands of school and American society without sacrificing the culture of the family or the authority structure that accompanies it. Hence there is little dissonance between the demands and expectations of school and family. For Mexican and Haitian children of immigrants, on the other hand, the existence of large, downtrodden coethnic communities can be worse than no community at all. These children enter into ready contact with peers who have already established an oppositional subculture that rejects the values of their traditional families and of the school. In contrast, the children of Mexican immigrants who continued to refer to themselves as "Mexicano," as opposed to Chicano or Mexican American, and characterized themselves as more closely

linked to the parental culture were among the most successful in
school. As Portes and Zhou note:

> Children of non-white immigrants may not even have the
> opportunity of gaining access to middle class white society,
> no matter how acculturated they become. Joining those na-
> tive circles to which they do have access may prove a ticket
> to permanent subordination and disadvantage. Remaining
> securely ensconced in their coethnic community, under
> these circumstances, may be not a symptom of escapism
> but the best strategy for capitalizing on otherwise unavail-
> able material and moral resources. . . . [A] strategy of
> paced, selective assimilation may prove the best course for
> immigrant minorities (1993: 96).

Thus Portes and Zhou, echoing in part the earlier work of Ogbu and
Matute-Bianchi, locate the problem of chronic underachievement of
Mexican American children within the structure of coethnic peer
communities that absorb succeeding generations of Mexican-origin
children not into the mainstream, but into an "adversarial stance of
impoverished groups confined to the bottom of the new economic
hourglass" (1993: 85).

While new immigrant students who are still tied to their native
cultures often outperform even students who were born in the United
States (Portes and Rumbaut 1994), most Chicano students have long
since left behind the immigrant mentality that might have protected
them from the competing force of an oppositional subculture (Macías
1993). And though Chicano students also tend to have high academic
and occupational *aspirations* (Portes and Rumbaut 1993), ironically
they quickly accommodate to the low education levels and menial
jobs that are the legacy of generations of Chicanos before them.

While these theories have been helpful in defining the problem—
and each holds some explanatory power[2]—they have done little to
remediate it. One strategy that researchers have advanced as a central
means for combating this problem is empowerment: empowering
parents to be advocates for their children (Delgado-Gaitán 1990), empowering communities to change their schools (Trueba 1988), and
empowering students to reconceptualize their own self-image as
learners (Gándara 1993). What all of these alternatives hold in common is an emphasis on the strengths that exist within these ethnic

---

[2] I would argue that while none of these theories can fully explain the
underachievement of Latino students, each contributes a partial understanding of the
problem. Even the deficit hypothesis, which was based on a Eurocentric and middle-
class view of sociocultural difference, provides some explanatory power when seen
from the perspective of the effects of poverty on the welfare of children and
communities.

communities but are rarely tapped. A number of interventions that build on the strengths of Latino students and families have been initiated in California; several of them operate in San Diego County.

Key Interventions That Address the Problem
Bilingual Education

The majority of Latino students in California are not immigrants and are primarily English-speaking. Nonetheless, English-language proficiency remains a major issue for the large numbers of Latino students who are either immigrants or the children of immigrants, and who still speak primarily Spanish in the home. In California, between 1.2 and 1.3 million students, the great majority of whom are Latinos from Mexico, are categorized as either limited-English or non-English-speaking and in need of specialized language assistance. Since 1976, some form of bilingual education has been the policy response to this need. Many smaller studies (such as Willig 1985) and one recent large study (Ramírez 1992) have shown that when limited-English students are provided with *good* bilingual instruction, they perform as well, and often better, than other limited-English and even native-English students. Yet the majority of limited-English-proficient students have not received a bilingual education, in this state or any other (Rumbaut and Cornelius 1995). The major reason for this has been a protracted political battle over the role of non-English languages in American society and the right of all students to have equal access to the school curriculum.

The greatest value of bilingual instruction, however, may well lie in its support for primary-language literacy activities within the home. The old admonishment to Latino parents not to speak Spanish to their children because it would impede their English acquisition has been thoroughly discredited, and we now know that speaking the native language in the home may in fact be key to the children's success in school. Literacy, the cornerstone of all educational development, results from exposure not only to the printed word but to the value of words, discussion, verbal exchange, and information (Goodman and Goodman 1990). And families can best nurture literacy in the language in which they are most comfortable and proficient. In fact, it is difficult to imagine nurturing a love of language and the printed word in an idiom one only partially comprehends or in which one has never read. Yet language policy in schools that reject bilingual education demands exactly this. Likewise, policies that have sought to immerse young children in English in the preschool or kindergarten in order to prepare them for all-English instruction have missed the message that parents are a child's first teachers. To the

extent that the parental role is undermined by instruction that alien-
ates the child from communication with the non-English-speaking
parent, not only is literacy placed at risk but so are parental authority
and important families ties (Wong-Fillmore 1991). Thus, in the preschool and elementary years, bilingual education has been the most
important educational intervention to aid Latino youths (and their
families) whose English skills are limited. In my research with Chicanos from low-income families who are exceptionally successful in
school, I have found that literacy training in the home, usually in
Spanish, was often the impetus for a life-long love of reading and
study (Gándara 1995).

Desegregation Efforts

There is substantial evidence that minority students who attend primarily minority (racially and ethnically isolated) schools do not perform as well as minority students who attend more racially integrated
schools (Orfield and Paul 1988; Jencks and Meyer 1990). Much of the
difference in achievement in these schools has been attributed to the
fact that they tend to be relatively less well funded and to have less
experienced and less capable teachers (ETS 1991; Espinosa and Ochoa
1995). However, the internal dynamics of schools and the student
composition can also have powerful effects on student achievement
and aspirations (Coleman et al. 1966). In my research, I have found
that desegregated school settings may contribute significantly to
positive outcomes for low-income Chicano achievers in several ways:
because the overall standards and offerings of the school may be
higher; because for many ambitious Chicano students these schools
provide the reassurance that they have done well in a highly competitive environment, thereby allowing them to envision themselves
surviving in a mostly Anglo university; and because low-income Latino students are able to access information through middle-income
Anglo students that otherwise would not be available to them within
their own social groups. The words of one young Chicana who had
been tracked into non–college preparatory classes in her high school
represent the experience of many whom I have interviewed:

> It was in band. As a result of being with the white students,
> having to sit next to them . . . I learned a lot about the aca-
> demic situation and how I wasn't reading Steinbeck, how I
> wasn't reading novels, and how I wasn't taking the same
> course that my peers were taking. That was real instructive
> to me, figuring out I had to take chemistry, so I did that on
> my own. . . . I would say that had the biggest impact, being

> in the band and seeing what I wasn't getting from school
> (Gándara 1995: 102).

Because this young Chicana was attending a mostly Anglo school with good resources and course selections, she could take the courses that allowed her to excel and eventually become a professor at a major university. Of the high-achieving Chicanos I have studied, between 70 and 80 percent did not attend the mostly minority schools to which they had been assigned; they and their families found ways out of the ethnic isolation in which they were raised. One strategy has long been to attend Catholic schools; other strategies include bussing to a non–minority school and attending a magnet school.

With increased racial isolation in urban areas and the complicity of the courts (Kunen 1996), many school districts have abandoned efforts at desegregation. This is painfully illustrated by data showing that Latino students are now more racially/ethnically isolated in their schools than at any other time in their history (Orfield 1993). One of the few remaining desegregation strategies in many areas is magnet schooling, developed to attract diverse groups of students from throughout a district. However, the ability of a child to attend a magnet school is predicated on available transportation and, for elementary school children, often on after-school childcare arrangements that can be coordinated with this plan. Moreover, many magnet schools have admissions criteria that effectively eliminate large portions of low-achieving minority children.

Reducing Dropout Rates

Larson and Rumberger (1995) point out that Latino students are unique, at least in the way they respond to school and particularly in the high rates at which they drop out of school. Hispanics have the highest dropout rates of all major ethnic groups, and Mexican Americans have the highest dropout rates of all Hispanics. Given that California Hispanics are overwhelmingly Mexican American, this accounts for the acute problem California schools face in retaining Latino students. Clearly, interventions are needed that reflect the particular needs of this population.

In attempting to address the dropout problem among Latino students, Larson and Rumberger have taken a comprehensive view of what they see as a complex web of factors contributing to dropout behavior. They point out that Latino students who drop out of school tend to begin this process early; they are more than twice as likely as Euro-Americans to drop out of school before the ninth grade. These students commonly lack social and task-oriented problem-solving skills. That is, they tend to have more difficulty with teachers and greater numbers of disciplinary problems than other students. They also tend to lack a sense of bonding with the school and generally feel alienated from the school environment. And they evidence high truancy prior to dropping out of school. Latino students who are at risk for dropping out need frequent and consistent feedback; quarterly report cards are not sufficient to monitor students who are not "on track" in school, and parents of these students need more information about how to manage their children and how to interact with the schools to benefit them. Finally, Larson and Rumberger note that low-income Latino parents often do not know where to turn for help, and they receive fragmented and inadequate social services which do not meet the basic needs of the family and hence make the job of parenting much more difficult.

Given these observations culled from a large body of literature, these researchers designed a dropout prevention program—ALAS, or Achievement for Latinos through Academic Success—targeted to Latino middle school students from low-income homes. The program uses a comprehensive and integrated approach to dropout prevention and incorporates six core steps in it strategy:

- Strengthen the students' social and task-related problem-solving skills.
- Provide recognition and bonding activities.
- Maintain intensive attendance monitoring.
- Provide frequent teacher feedback to the parent and the student.
- Teach parents school participation and teen management.
- Integrate school and home needs with community services.

Using this integrated approach with Latino students in a large urban middle school in Los Angeles, Larson and Rumberger have been able to reduce student dropout significantly,[3] registering a 43 percent improvement. They have also been successful in reducing excessive absenteeism, raising grade point averages, and increasing unit credits of the program students in comparison to a randomly selected control group of students from the same school.

---

[3] Here the term "mobility" is most appropriate since it is not always possible to know if students have indeed dropped out of school altogether, or simply moved. Nonetheless, high mobility is also a precursor to dropping out and therefore is to be discouraged for its own sake.

INCREASING THE POOL OF POST-SECONDARY STUDENTS

Reducing dropout rates and increasing high school graduation rates are important steps in plugging the leaks in the pipeline. But also important is stimulating the pool of students who will perform well enough and be motivated to go on to college. This problem is the target of two programs operating in San Diego County and throughout California: AVID and Puente.

AVID, or Advancement Via Individual Determination, takes a comprehensive approach to stimulating the pool of students eligible for college, but it is not quite as comprehensive as the ALAS program. In part, this is because the students it selects are not as "high risk" as the ALAS students; these students must demonstrate high potential, generally through test scores that are at the fourth stanine and above, and with grade point averages that do not dip below a C. AVID targets low-income students, though it does not focus on a particular ethnic group. It describes itself as an "untracking" intervention in which students who would probably not otherwise have been "tracked" into the college preparatory courses are placed in them along with a special elective class that focuses on developing academic skills through tutoring, test-taking and note-taking skills, college information seminars and field trips, and direct help in filling out college applications.

Mehan, Hubbard, and Villanueva (1994) have studied the effects of this program on Latino students in the San Diego area. In order to be included in the study, students had to have attended AVID classes for three years. Mehan and his colleagues found that AVID Latino students were attending four-year colleges at a much higher rate than Latino students as a group in the San Diego schools: 44 percent versus 25 percent. Moreover, the AVID program had included students whose mean family income was considerably lower than that for the district as a whole. The researchers point out that the AVID program is able to do many of the things for these students that their parents are not able to do, because of low levels of education, inadequate resources, or a lack of knowledge regarding how to manipulate the system. AVID essentially is an advocate for the students while providing them with a "scaffolding," or support system, that allows them to succeed in college preparatory classes. Because it does not target the higher risk students, its focus is more narrow than the Puente program, described below, which also attempts to stimulate the pool of college-bound Latinos.

The Puente program, which also has sites in the San Diego area, targets the full range of students, from high risk to high potential. It takes a comprehensive approach and limits itself to a single target group: Latinos. The High School Puente program is based on a highly successful community college program operating in California since

1982. It presently has thirty-two junior college and eighteen high school sites. In a study of twenty-three Puente-participating community colleges, compared to twenty-three non-Puente colleges, the Latino Eligibility Study found that the Puente colleges transferred 44 percent more Latino students into four-year universities (LES 1993b).

Like AVID, the High School Puente project is an "untracking" program in that it assigns students, many of whom would otherwise be relegated to non–college preparatory courses, into the college-prep track while providing the support and infrastructure to help them succeed in those classes. Unlike AVID, many of the Puente students are not high performers on standardized tests. In fact, these very tests have, in many cases, led to the perception that they are not "college material." Puente has three major components: freshman and sophomore English classes that focus on intensive writing instruction and an introduction to Chicano/Latino literature; a counselor assigned to each student; and a mentor from the Latino community.

Enthusiasm among parents is high (82 percent express strong approval of the program), and students have shown a strong commitment to it : 80 to 85 percent have remained with the program over two years, registering grade point averages and college preparatory credits that are significantly higher than other Latino students in the same school (see table 5.6). These early data are especially compelling given that the program has included students along the entire spectrum of achievement—from high achievers to those who are at risk for school failure—in approximately equal percentages.

TABLE 5.6
1993–94 PUENTE COHORT VS. NON-PUENTE LATINOS'
GPA AND UNITS EARNED

Term	Group	N	Regular GPA	Units Attempted	Units Earned
Ninth grade					
Fall	Puente	120	2.61	32	30
	Control	994	2.04	32	27
Spring	Puente	124	2.60	62	58
	Control	936	1.98	60	51
Tenth grade					
Fall	Puente	68	2.24	96	87
	Control	761	1.97	90	76

Also compelling is the extent to which Puente appears to provide a safe space for students to explore their multiple, sometimes competing, identities—the identity of *hijo* or *hija*, of homeboy or homegirl, and of academic achiever.

> [T]he program establishes a space where some students are able to begin to reconcile their multiple identities, including their notion of what ethnic identity means to them. This is best illustrated in a discussion of a take-home assignment in which the students were asked to interview their parents about how they identified themselves, that is, what ethnicity they aligned themselves with and why. Students openly shared their own responses as well as those of their parents; and some were in conflict. It became apparent that students were taking advantage of their opportunity to declare such unspoken feelings which are too often censored among their peers. It was obvious that such feelings emerged due to the "safe" environment that had been cultivated by the program (Quijada 1996).

MURALS

The Minority Undergraduate Research Apprenticeship in Letters & Sciences (MURALS) model program at the University of California, Davis campus and other campuses brings together ambitious Chicano and other minority students with faculty who can mentor them into academic careers. The program links these students at the pregraduate level with faculty mentors who sponsor them in research projects. Through exposure to research, hands-on experience, and close contact with the faculty member, students are able to learn what graduate education is all about and are given the opportunity to form a special relationship with their faculty mentor, something rarely available to undergraduates in our large institutions. This program can spark an interest in graduate education for students who, in all likelihood, would not have considered this option. While the final data are not in, preliminary results suggest that the program has been quite successful in propelling a number of students into graduate careers.

Latino Education and the Political Environment

One tension in the (generally successful) interventions implemented for Latino youths is that existing between programs that group students by ethnicity and those that seek to break down Latino isolation. While these approaches may be different, they are not necessarily in conflict. Bilingual education programs require a critical mass of

Spanish-speaking students for instruction in core subjects. Yet the best
of these programs also integrate these students with English-speaking
and non-Latino peers for significant portions of the day. Desegregation efforts seek to dismantle isolated enclaves of students within segregated schools and provide students with meaningful contact with
peers of different backgrounds, but nothing in these efforts suggests
that Latino students should spend all of their time with non-Latinos.
In fact, from my research it is clear that the most successful Chicano
students are those who are able to maintain friendship groups with
both Latino and non-Latino students. These are the students who have
learned how to move between cultures. They know

> how to handle themselves with high-achieving Anglos,
> and they [are] still equally comfortable in the company of
> friends who [will] never leave the fields, the barrios, or go
> to college. For the most part, they [are] able to make the
> jump into the mainstream, without alienating the com-
> munities from which they came. It is easy to see how this
> social adaptability could become a great advantage later in
> life, and a major factor in their continued academic success
> (Gándara 1995: 77).

Ironically, however, recent political events have put at risk both
the efforts to break down the isolation of Latino students and the
strategies that seek to group students to develop a positive identity
and deal with personal, challenging issues in a safe environment. As
Kunen (1996: 39) notes:

> [T]he high court's action [in dismantling the Kansas City
> desegregation plan] has accelerated the pace at which cities
> across the country are moving to undo mandatory *desegre-*
> gation. And the federal judiciary, which long staked its
> authority on the enforcement of desegregation orders, ap-
> pears eager to depart the field. Chris Hansen of the Ameri-
> can Civil Liberties Union in New York City observes, "The
> courts are saying, 'We still agree with the goal of desegre-
> gation, but it's too hard, and we're tired, and we give up.'"

At the same time that desegregation efforts are foundering across
the nation, California has been at the forefront of several new initiatives to make it illegal to acknowledge the race, ethnicity, or gender of
a person in decisions about job hires, college admissions, or provisions of government services of any kind, including education out-
reach programs. Legislation is also pending to completely dismantle
the state's bilingual education regulations and to bar illegal immigrants from any state services, including schooling.

The first of these initiatives—the California Civil Rights Initiative (CCRI) and what have become known as SP–1 and SP–2, resolutions passed by the University of California Board of Regents—might well make programs such as Puente, ALAS, and MURALS illegal because of the fact that they target *particular* students.[4] These initiatives claim to want to "level the playing field" by ignoring racial and ethnic backgrounds of people, as though these were characteristic that have no bearing on life chances or opportunities, a position that has been contradicted by mountains of social science research over the last half-century. The CCRI will be on the California ballot in November 1996. SP–1 and SP–2 passed the Board of Regents on July 20, 1995; how they are to be implemented remains the source of considerable legal and political wrangling.

A number of bills have been introduced in the California legislature, which is sharply divided along party lines, that would strip away language from the education code that provides for bilingual instruction for limited-English-proficient students. Whatever shape that legislation eventually takes, it is certain to reduce the regulatory safeguards for LEP students and ensure that more of them will receive exclusively English instruction despite the fact that this strategy has proven a failure in the past.

Title VII was enacted in 1968, and state legislation followed soon thereafter, as a response to the widely acknowledged fact that "language minority groups . . . have been subject to discrimination and limited opportunity. . . . [T]he public school does not appear to have met [their] needs" (United States Commission 1975). The commission contended in this report that a remedy must be found to guarantee equal access for children "who are unable to benefit from an exclusively English curriculum." That remedy was codified in the Bilingual Education Act of 1974, which stipulated that "such [bilingual] instruction shall, to the extent necessary, be in all courses or subjects of study which will allow a child to progress effectively through the educational system." Given that these mandates have never been fully acted upon and that large numbers of language-minority students in both California and the nation have never received the services that were specified in the twenty-year-old regulations, it is difficult to understand how returning to the days when no program was provided and children were left to "sink or swim" in English-only classrooms could possibly enhance the life chances of LEP students. But then, it is evident from the tone of other legislation

---

[4]The MURALS program changed its name in 1991 to Mentorships for Undergraduate Researchers in Agriculture, Letters & Sciences, removing the allusion to its minority focus in order to reduce its political visibility.

that enhancing the life chances of LEP students is hardly among these legislators' priority concerns.

Proposition 187, passed by California voters in November 1994, excludes undocumented or unauthorized immigrants from receiving most public services, including education. The initiative requires or encourages various state and local government officials to identify and report persons suspected of being unauthorized immigrants. Prop. 187 is currently tied up in the courts, however, because it violates various state and federal constitutions and *Plyler v. Doe*, in which the U.S. Supreme Court held in 1982 that immigrant children are entitled to "equal protection of the laws" and thus are not to be excluded from public schools. Nonetheless, if the initiative survives the various constitutional tests, in addition to barring undocumented immigrant children from the schools, it would have a very serious financial impact on schools in a state that already ranks forty-second in the nation with respect to support for public education (California Department of Education 1995). The California Department of Education has estimated that the potential impact on the statewide funding guarantee would be between $1.35 and $1.845 billion. Moreover, since California elementary and secondary schools currently receive approximately $2.3 billion in federal funding, this sum may also be in jeopardy if districts are forced to violate the Family Educational Right and Privacy Act (FERPA) by collecting protected information on students (California Department of Education 1994). The same directive adds that another $161 million in costs would be incurred in the first year to verify the immigration status of students in the schools. Clearly, if Proposition 187 were to pass constitutional tests, it would represent a financial debacle for the state's schools.

The financial ramifications of Proposition 187 for California schools would be devastating, but perhaps this is of lesser consequence than the proposition's impact on the climate of the state. As Cornelius so cogently notes,

> Given this climate of opinion, it was a natural progression
> to move from steps to reduce immigrants' access to basic
> human services (Proposition 187) to renewed attacks on
> bilingual education and other programs seen as benefiting
> immigrants and other minorities, and to attempts to create
> a more exclusionary concept of U.S. citizenship (1995: 9).

The effects of all of these policies on the Latino population are relatively clear. However, there are also consequences for society as a whole. As educational opportunity is diminished for Latinos and fewer and fewer students are able to navigate successfully through the pipeline, the California and national economies will pay in lost dollars and cents. A recent study by the Rand Corporation looked at

the economic consequences of raising the level of education for Hispanics. It concluded that:

> Hispanics with a bachelor's degree will pay more than
> twice as much in taxes as those with only a high school di-
> ploma, and Hispanics with a professional degree will pay
> an estimated three times as much as those with a bachelor's
> degree (Sorensen et al. 1995: 2–3).

Sorensen and his colleagues further compute that if Hispanic participation in higher education were raised to the level of Anglos for a
single cohort of students, this would result in a $30 billion increase in
federal tax payments and a $6.6 billion increase in contributions to
Social Security and Medicare. Failing to increase the educational attainment of Hispanics, however, "will exact a high economic toll for
individuals and for society. Given the experience of other underedu-
cated groups, there are certainly concomitant human, social and political costs" (p. 4).

Since issues of economic self-interest as well as social justice point
to the conclusion that we must find ways to increase the educational
attainment of Latinos, what policies might lead to such an outcome?

Education and Social Policy Recommendations

• *The schools must nurture literacy in Latino students and families.*

Defined as exposure not only to the printed word but also to the
value of words, discussion, verbal exchange, and information, literacy
is the key to students' academic engagement in any language. Families can best nurture literacy in the language in which they are most
comfortable and proficient. Hence literacy activities in the school
should incorporate the language of the student's family and be con-
structed to allow the family to participate in these activities. Bilingual
instruction is not just an important means of providing limited-
English-proficient students with access to the core curriculum while
they learn English; it is also an important means of keeping the family
linked to the learning of the child. In this way, even students who appear to be proficient in English but whose parents are not can be
aided by literacy activities that take into account the language of the
home.

• *Schools should not give up on desegregation.*

As urban areas around the country have been abandoned by the
middle class and Anglo residents who formerly inhabited them, efforts to desegregate many school districts have been stymied. Recent

court decisions as well as public discussion have turned to the idea of strengthening racially segregated schools rather than dwelling on the difficult task of desegregating them. And many responsible educators have advocated putting resources that might otherwise be devoted to desegregation efforts into building high-quality, all-minority schools, arguing that the critical variable is school excellence, not the students' racial or ethnic mix. Bilingual educators have also worried over the need to maintain a critical mass of limited-English-proficient students in a single language at the same school site in order to provide adequate primary-language instruction. These are both important goals, but the data point to the need to exercise extreme caution when creating or maintaining all-minority environments.

Excellent minority schools may equip students with the skills they need to continue their educations beyond high school, but they will not provide the validation that comes from competing in an arena that mirrors the society into which they will be thrust. Neither do such homogeneous settings prepare students to move gracefully between one social context and another, as any successful inhabitant of twenty-first-century North America will need to do. My research subjects have commented repeatedly on how their self-concept was enhanced by knowing they could compete successfully against high schools peers whom they viewed as being models of achievement. It was this knowledge and confidence that allowed them to imagine themselves in a world-class university. Moreover, there is considerable evidence that moving back and forth between the two cultures— home peer groups and school peer groups—provides important adaptive skills that increase chances of persisting in school.

Although to a large degree decisions about school desegregation have been the purview of the federal courts, education reformers must not remain silent on this issue. Local and state education policies can—and, some would argue, should—address the need for and the wisdom of providing racially and ethnically integrating experiences as part of the school curriculum. Perhaps the linkages will occur over fiber-optic cables rather than bus routes, as in an experiment conducted by Sayers (Cummins and Sayers 1995) in which children of different ethnicities were linked from coast to coast via the Internet to work together on projects that helped to break down stereotypes about each other. However this is achieved, the evidence suggests that minority students, and more particularly Chicano students, are advantaged by sitting next to students who consider it their birthright to go to college.

- *We must find ways to put resources into programs that address the complex needs of Chicano students.*

As Larson and Rumberger (1995) have found, dropping out of school is not a simple phenomenon of a student deciding one day that she no longer wants to go to school. These are complex decisions that result from many factors, often related to family conditions. The only way to seriously stem the dropping out of Latino youths is to intervene early and intensively in their lives, to provide support for parents as well as students, and to monitor them carefully to ensure they don't slip through the cracks. While this is expensive, when compared with doing nothing, it is cheap. The loss to the economy when students do not complete school and remain only tentatively linked to the labor force is far greater than the cost of a social worker. At the upper ends of the education continuum, every Latino who completes college or graduate school more than pays back the education subsidy in taxes paid over a lifetime.

- *We must find ways to "untrack" students who demonstrate interest and/or potential in continuing their studies.*

Tracking also is a complex phenomenon and is not easily attacked in a monolithic way. Removing all groupings of students would not necessarily solve many of the problems of access for Latino students. Mehan, Hubbard, and Villanueva (1994) allude to the fact that their AVID experiment was not a "radical" reform in that it did not dismantle all tracking in the schools; it simply removed from the lower tracks students who showed some potential for postsecondary study. Yet it is quite probable that had these researchers attempted the "radical" approach, their efforts would not have been as well rewarded.

The whole issue of academic tracking is more complex than educators have fully acknowledged. Its evils, painfully documented, have caused many to renounce it as a policy, at the same time that teachers, pointing out their frustration in trying to teach algebra to students who cannot add, have caused these same educators to rethink their renunciations.

Tracking works for some students. It worked for the students in the AVID and Puente programs; it provides the environment, the encouragement, the peer group, knowledge of the subject matter, and the real-world information that is critical in propelling them forward. It also isolates them to some extent from peers who are headed down a different path. Were these students heterogeneously grouped with their neighborhood peers, it is entirely possible that their life and academic choices would be quite different. Yet they represent only a small percentage of their social and economic peer group, and, by their own admissions, they are often not the brightest stars, even in their own local galaxies.

Education reform must grapple with the conundrum of academic tracking and find a way to wrap at-risk students who aspire to a different future in a protective, college-bound cocoon, while still providing access to these same opportunities for students who may not yet know they want to, or can, reach that far.

- *We must find ways to reward persistence over measured "ability" in Latino students.*

While the American educational system is no doubt the most open in the world with respect to providing access, there is something in the American ethos that is more powerful than structural barriers in precluding higher academic attainment. This is the unspoken belief in the salience of ability over effort which results in our willingness to turn over the futures of our children to the assumed predictive ability of standardized tests.

Students in the AVID and Puente programs had been "untracked." That is, many of them would not have been placed in college preparatory classes had the programs not intervened on their behalf. In my research, I have consistently found that about 20 percent of exceptionally high achieving Latinos had originally been assigned to non–college preparatory coursework, usually on the basis of a low standardized test score. Ironically, the AVID program uses standardized test scores to identify students with relatively low GPAs who might, nonetheless, do well enough in high school to pursue college. But because Latinos typically score about three-quarters of a standard deviation below Anglo students on major standardized tests, more often than not the test scores become a reason to deny them opportunities rather than opening new doors. Even in the face of high academic achievement, counselors often place more faith in the test scores than they do in a student's actual performance.

One well-known teacher who has had extraordinary success with Chicano students from low-income backgrounds tells his high school administration, "Don't send me 'gifted' kids; I want kids who want to become gifted. In my class they will become gifted!" Then he asks the students, "Who wants to study? Who wants to work hard? Who wants a ticket to college?"[5] Into this self-selected group fall many students whom other teachers have written off because of low grades or test scores. And, incredibly, they "become gifted," not by fiat but by investing more time and effort in the subject matter than other students.

Assessment will no doubt command a larger and larger role in our education reform efforts; it is important to monitor our progress. Nonetheless we must find ways to monitor without presorting. Test-

---

[5] Quotes from Jaime Escalante's classroom, fall 1992.

ing and assessment of *individual* students must be reconceptualized as diagnostic, not predictive, and a student's, and family's, willingness to put forth effort should always be the primary factor in awarding opportunity. This is an important principle for all students, but it becomes especially key for Chicano students who have been tripped up time and again by formal and informal assessments that have plainly underestimated their potential and too often led to inappropriate tracking decisions.

- *We should extend programs such as MURALS to all university campuses and charge all faculty with the responsibility of helping underrepresented students to envision a graduate education, and perhaps even a career as a university professor.*

If we are to have any hope of diversifying the professoriate, it will require a concerted effort on the part of faculty to make this happen. Chicano students do not come to college planning to become university professors. In my research on high-achieving Chicanos from low-income backgrounds, I never encountered an undergraduate student who set out to have a career in academia. This almost always happens as a result of an intense and positive experience with a particular professor. University faculty must accept this challenge.

- *Within the political limitations that exist, we must find ways to target particular students who, because of their unique backgrounds, require interventions that are tailored to their particular needs.*

Students do not all share the same histories or conditions. As much as some would like for it to be so, the playing field is *not* level, and all students do not bring the same resources to the educational experience. We must find ways to acknowledge this fact and treat students *differently* in order that their life chances might be the same. We have heard from students who participate in the Puente program how important it is for them to have a "safe place" where they can deal with issues of identity, aspirations, and skills without fear of ridicule from students who do not share their particular circumstances. Programs like Puente, which provide a safe haven for students, or ALAS, which reach out to the particular needs of low-income, often immigrant, Spanish-speaking families, or MURALS, which provide the kind of critical relationship with faculty members that minority students rarely have the confidence to seek, might not exist under the provisions of the CCRI or SP–1. Yet such programs may well be key to moving many Latino students through the educational pipeline.

References

Aguirre, Adalberto, Jr., and Rubén O. Martínez. 1993. *Chicanos in Higher Education: Issues and Dilemmas for the 21st Century.* Washington, D.C.: School of Education and Human Development, George Washington University.

Bourdieu, Pierre, and Jean-Claude Passeron. 1977. *Reproduction in Education, Society and Culture.* Beverly Hills, Calif.: Sage.

Bowles, Samuel, and Herbert Gintis. 1976. *Schooling in Capitalist America: Educational Reform and the Contradictions of Economic Life.* New York: Basic Books.

Buenning, M., and Nona Tollefson. 1987. "The Cultural Gap Hypothesis as an Explanation for the Achievement Patterns of Mexican-American Students," *Psychology in the Schools* 24: 264–72.

California Department of Finance. 1996. *K–12 Graded Public School Enrollment by Ethnicity, History and Projection—1995 Series.* Sacramento, Calif.: DOF.

Carter, Thomas P., and Roberto D. Segura. 1979. *Mexican Americans in School: Decade of Change.* 2d ed. New York: College Entrance Examination Board.

CDE (California Department of Education). 1994. Memorandum to County and District Superintendents, Analysis of Proposition 187, September 7. Sacramento: CDE.

————. 1995. *Fingertip Facts on Education in California.* Sacramento, Calif.: CDE.

————. 1996. *Language Census, 1996.* Sacramento, Calif.: CDE.

Coleman, James S., et al. 1966. *Equality of Educational Opportunity.* Washington, D.C.: U.S. Government Printing Office.

Cornelius, Wayne A. 1995. "Educating California's Immigrant Children: Introduction and Overview." In *California's Immigrant Children: Theory, Research, and Implications for Educational Policy,* edited by Rubén G. Rumbaut and Wayne A. Cornelius. La Jolla: Center for U.S.–Mexican Studies, University of California, San Diego.

Cummins, Jim, and Dennis Sayers. 1995. *Brave New Schools: Challenging Cultural Illiteracy through Global Learning Networks.* New York: St. Martin's Press.

De La Rosa, Denise, and Carlyle E. Maw. 1990. *Hispanic Education: A Statistical Portrait 1990.* Washington, D.C.: National Council of La Raza.

Delgado-Gaitán, Concha. 1990. *Literacy for Empowerment: The Role of Parents in Children's Education.* London: Falmer Press.

Espinosa, Rubén, and Alberto Ochoa. 1995. "The Educational Attainment of California Youth: A Research Note." In *Changing Schools for Changing Students,* edited by Reynaldo Macías and Reyna Guadalupe García Ramos. Santa Barbara: Linguistic Minority Research Institute, University of California.

ETS (Educational Testing Service). 1991. *The State of Inequality.* Princeton, N.J.: ETS.

Fernández, Roberto, and Gerald Shu. 1988. "School Dropouts: New Approaches to an Enduring Problem," *Education and Urban Society* 20: 363–86.

Gándara, Patricia. 1986. *Bilingual Education: Learning English in California.* Sacramento, Calif.: Assembly Office of Research.

————. 1993. "Language and Ethnicity as Factors in School Failure: The Case of Mexican Americans." In *Children at Risk in America: History, Concepts, and Public Policy*, edited by Robert Wollons. New York: State University of New York Press.

————. 1995. *Over the Ivy Walls: The Educational Mobility of Low Income Chicanos*. Albany: State University of New York Press.

Gibson, Margaret A. 1988. *Accommodation without Assimilation: Sikh Immigrants in an American High School*. New York: Cornell University Press.

Giroux, Henry A. 1983. *Theory and Resistance: A Pedagogy for the Opposition*. South Hadley, Mass.: Bergin and Garvey.

Goodman, Yetta M., and Kenneth S. Goodman. 1990. "Vygotsky in a Whole Language Perspective." In *Vygotsky and Education: Instructional Implications and Applications of Sociohistorical Psychology*, edited by Luis C. Moll. New York: Cambridge University Press.

Hess, Robert D., and V. Shipman. 1965. "Early Experience and the Socialization of Cognitive Modes in Children," *Child Development* 36: 869–86.

Hymes, Dell. 1974. *Foundations in Sociolinguistics: An Ethnographic Approach*. Philadelphia: University of Pennsylvania Press.

Jencks, Christopher, and Susan Meyer. 1990. "The Social Consequences of Growing Up in a Poor Neighborhood." In *Innercity Poverty in the United States*, edited by Laurence E. Lynee and Michael McGeary. Washington, D.C.: National Academy Press.

Kunen, J. 1996. "The End of Integration," *Time* 147 (18): 38–45.

Lareau, Annette. 1987. "Social Class Differences in Family–School Relationships: The Importance of Cultural Capital," *Sociology of Education* 60: 73–85.

————. 1989. *Home Advantage: Social Class and Parental Intervention in Elementary Education*. London and New York: Falmer Press.

Larson, Katherine, and Russell Rumberger. 1995. "Doubling School Success in Highest-risk Latino Youth: Results from a Middle School Intervention Study." In *Changing Schools for Changing Students*, edited by Reynaldo Macías and Reyna Guadalupe García Ramos. Santa Barbara: Linguistic Minority Research Institute, University of California.

LES (Latino Eligibility Study). 1993a. *Report Number One*. Santa Cruz: Regents of the University of California, University of California, Santa Cruz.

————. 1993b. *Report Number Two*. Santa Cruz: Regents of the University of California, University of California, Santa Cruz.

Macías, Reynaldo. 1993. "Language and Ethnic Classification of Language Minorities: Chicano and Latino Students in the 1990s," *Hispanic Journal of Behavioral Science* 15: 230–57.

MacLeod, Jay. 1995. *Ain't No Making It: Aspirations and Attainment in a Low-income Neighborhood*. Boulder, Colo.: Westview.

Matute-Bianchi, Maria E. 1986. "Ethnic Identities and Patterns of School Success and Failure among Mexican-descent and Japanese American Students in a California High School," *American Journal of Education* 95: 233–55.

Mehan, Hugh. 1992. "Understanding Inequality in Schools: The Contribution of Interpretive Studies," *Sociology of Education* 65: 1–20.

Mehan, Hugh, L. Hubbard, and I. Villanueva. 1994. "Forming Academic Identities: Accommodation without Assimilation among Involuntary Minorities," *Anthropology and Education Quarterly* 25: 91–117.

NCES (National Center for Education Statistics). 1995a. *The Educational Progress of Hispanic Students.* Washington, D.C.: Office of Educational Research and Improvement, U.S. Department of Education.

———. 1995b. *National Assessment of Educational Progress.* Washington, D.C.: Office of Educational Research and Improvement, U.S. Department of Education.

Ogbu, John. 1987. "Variability in Minority School Performance: A Problem in Search of an Explanation," *Anthropology and Education Quarterly* 18: 312–34.

Ogbu, John, and Maria Matute-Bianchi. 1986. "Understanding Sociocultural Factors: Knowledge, Identity, and School Adjustment." In *Beyond Language: Social and Cultural Factors in Schooling Language Minority Students.* Los Angeles: Evaluation, Dissemination, and Assessment Center, California State University, Los Angeles.

Orfield, Gary. 1993. *The Growth of Segregation in American Schools: Changing Patterns of Separation and Poverty since 1968.* Alexandria, Va: National School Boards Association.

Orfield, Gary, and Faith Paul. 1988. "Declines in Minority Access: A Tale of Five Cities," *Educational Record* 68 (4): 56–62.

PACE (Policy Analysis for California Education). 1995. *The Condition of Education in California, 1994–95.* Berkeley: PACE.

Phillips, Kevin P. 1990. *The Politics of Rich and Poor: Wealth and the American Electorate in the Reagan Aftermath.* New York: Random House.

Portes, Alejandro, and Rubén Rumbaut. 1993. "The Assimilation Process of Children of Immigrants." Release No. 1, The Children of Immigrants Project. Baltimore, Md.: Johns Hopkins University.

———. 1994. "The Educational Progress of Children of Immigrants." Release No. 2, The Children of Immigrants Project. Baltimore, Md.: Johns Hopkins University.

Portes, Alejandro, and Min Zhou. 1993. "The New Second Generation: Segmented Assimilation and Its Variants," *Annals of the American Academy of Political and Social Science* 530: 75–96.

Quijada, David. 1996. "Reconciling Multiple Identities: Latino Student Experiences in a College Prep Program." Paper presented at the American Educational Research Association Conference, New York, April 12.

Ramírez, J. David. 1992. "Executive Summary," *Bilingual Research Journal* 16: 1–62.

Rumbaut, Rubén G., and Wayne A. Cornelius, eds. 1995. *California's Immigrant Children: Theory, Research, and Implications for Educational Policy.* U.S.–Mexican Contemporary Perspectives Series, no. 8. La Jolla: Center for U.S.–Mexican Studies, University of California, San Diego.

Rumberger, Russell. 1991. "Chicano Dropouts: A Review of Research and Policy Issues." In *Chicano School Failure and Success: Research and Policy Agendas for the 1990s,* edited by Richard R. Valencia. New York: Falmer Press.

Sorensen, Seymour, et al. 1995. "Increasing Hispanic Participation in Higher Education: A Desirable Public Investment." Issue paper of the Institute on Education and Training. Santa Monica, Calif.: RAND.

Trueba, Henry T. 1988. "Culturally Based Explanations of Minority Students' Educational Achievement," *Anthropology and Education Quarterly* 19: 270–87.

United States Commission on Civil Rights. 1975. *A Better Chance to Learn: Bilingual Bicultural Education.* Washington, D.C.: The Commission.

Valentine, Charles A. 1968. *Culture and Poverty, Critique and Counter-proposals.* Chicago, Ill: University of Chicago Press.

Willig, Ann C. 1985. "A Meta-analysis of Selected Studies on the Effectiveness of Bilingual Education," *Review of Educational Research* 55: 269–317.

Willis, Paul E. 1977. *Learning to Labor: How Working Class Kids Get Working Class Jobs.* New York: Columbia University Press.

Wong-Fillmore, Lily. 1991. "When Learning a Second Language Means Losing the First," *Early Childhood Research Quarterly* 6: 323–47.

6

Migration and Ethnic Politics in a Transnational Age: Reflections on the California–Mexico Border

David G. Gutiérrez

Latino immigrants have recently emerged as a favorite target in the rhetoric of professional politicians, from the neo-nativistic pronouncements of Pat Buchanan to the more tempered, yet somehow more disturbing, restrictionist sentiments expressed by supposed liberals like Senators Dianne Feinstein and Barbara Boxer of California (see, for example, Bornemeier 1993; Braun and Fulwood 1996; Bunting and Miller 1993). Of course, the figure who has been most successful at manipulating the immigration issue for political advantage is Governor Pete Wilson of California. Although his attempt to ride the issue to the White House ultimately failed, Wilson and other like-minded public figures have been extremely effective in mobilizing popular support for aggressive federal action to "regain control of the nation's borders" and to deny public services such as health care and education to undocumented residents and their children (see Stall and McDonnell 1993; Weintraub 1994; Wilson 1994). Indeed, so efficient have been such efforts to demonize "illegal aliens" that much of the public seems now to believe that undocumented migrants caught in the United States deserve whatever fate befalls them (see Goldman, Malnic, and Weinstein 1996; letters to editor, *Los Angeles Times*, March 27, April 1, May 13, 1996).

Analysts are divided about how to interpret recent developments in the immigration debate. Some observers tend to view the current period of anti-immigrant sentiment as merely the latest flare-up in a long line of American nativist outbursts. From this point of view, the most recent cycle of nativism will probably cause a brief period of public reassessment of the issue, followed by a new round of immigration policy reform. Others, including this author, tend to see this immigration crisis from a fundamentally different vantage point. Rather than assuming that the current situation is merely one more iteration, which, like its predecessors, will be "solved" through some combination of policy reform, compromise, and mollification of the voting public, a growing number of immigration scholars and activists have suggested that we are witnessing the results of a series of much more profound changes in the nature of migration patterns. Drawing on insights generated by linking recent transnational migration trends and the upsurge of nativism in the United States, this chapter attempts to analyze and situate historically the current public debate over immigration politics in San Diego, in Southern California, and, by extension, in the western United States.

The Tortured Construction of the Debate

In Los Angeles I recently came upon a group of men standing on a street corner, clearly part of the pool of "casual laborers" that has become ubiquitous in Southern California's social landscape. These individuals represent the most recent illustration of a 100–year, virtually uninterrupted history of Spanish-speaking men (and sometimes women) gathering on urban street corners, outside of hardware stores and nurseries, near construction sites, or along roadsides adjacent to fields and orchards. First drawn in the late nineteenth century to jobs in the Southwest's rapidly expanding economy, and later recruited under the auspices of various formal and informal foreign-labor importation schemes, Mexican migrant laborers gradually became a crucial component of the American labor market.

Although much of the early migratory flow was cyclical in nature, over time more and more Mexican migrants "settled out" of the migrant stream to establish permanent homes in the United States. Census data amply illustrate this phenomenon: whereas the total ethnic Mexican population (including both Americans of Mexican descent and resident Mexican nationals) of the United States was probably no more than 400,000 or 500,000 in 1900, by the late 1920s at least 1.5 million Mexicans had migrated into the United States. Although many of these early migrants were returned to Mexico during the infamous repatriation campaigns of the Great Depression, this first group provided the demographic foundation for the growth of the modern Mexican American population of the United States (see Hernández 1966; Boswell 1979; Corwin 1978).

In recent decades, migration from Mexico and other Latin American nations has increased exponentially. For example, in 1960, the nation's ethnic Mexican population stood at only 3.5 million; it rose to 4.5 million in 1970, 8.7 million in 1980, and 13.4 million by 1990. Growth rates for the "Latino" or pan-Hispanic population of the United States (that is, the combined population of persons of South American, Central American, and Hispanic Caribbean descent residing in the United States) were similar in magnitude. The aggregate Latino population grew from about 7 million in 1960 to 10.5 million in 1970 and 14.6 million in 1980. By 1994 the U.S. population of Latino descent was estimated to be in excess of 27 million people (Bean and Tienda 1987; Lorey 1990; Martin and Midgley 1994; U.S. Bureau of the Census 1991; Weeks and Ham-Chande 1992). In California, rates of growth of the Latino population (mostly of Mexican descent) were similar. From a population of less than 1.5 million in 1960, California's Latino population grew to 2.14 million in 1970, 4.57 million in 1980, and more than 9 million in 1990 (Hayes-Bautista, Schink, and Chapa 1988: 26). By 1996 nearly one in three of all Californians was of Latino descent. If current trends continue, demographers estimate that almost half (49.7 percent) of all Californians will be of Latino descent by the year 2040 (Rosenblatt 1996).

On some levels Californians, residents of the Southwest, and other Americans are well aware that this demographic revolution has altered many aspects of regional life. Indeed, for residents of Los Angeles County in particular, but for other locales as well, it is impossible *not* to recognize that Latinos have become a major presence, if not an actual majority, in many communities; that ethnic Mexican and other Latino migrants have for years been the backbone of the labor force in the agricultural, garment, restaurant, electronics assembly, and domestic service industries; and that they are an important presence in the construction, janitorial, maintenance, and other sectors based on the use of casual and less than full-time labor.

However, on other levels, Californians and other residents of the Southwest have exhibited a peculiar inability to "see" the ethnic Mexicans and other Latinos who live among them. This curious myopia has deep and complicated roots in the region's past. Growing both out of the social polarization caused by years of residential segregation and out of Anglo Americans' remarkable capacity to maintain a romanticized (and sanitized) memory of the American Southwest's Hispanic past, this self-induced near-sightedness has long allowed residents of the region to pretend that Latinos are not an integral part of American society. Over the course of many years, this social myopia has not only effaced or grossly distorted the history of Latinos in the United States, but it has also materially contributed to the construction and perpetuation of one-sided popular analyses of the immigration controversy (Gutiérrez 1996; Thomas 1991).

Nowhere has this myopia been more apparent than at the level of political discourse and debate. Although it has been increasingly difficult for politicians operating in the U.S.–Mexico border region not to acknowledge the importance of the increasing integration of the regional economies (particularly after ratification of the North American Free Trade Agreement in 1993), most have remained remarkably adept at keeping economic and trade issues separate from questions of transnational labor migration (see Acevedo and Espenshade 1992; Sassen 1990). Similarly, although most politicians are aware that the interests and demands of American citizens of Latino descent can no longer be ignored in the way they were, say, in the 1940s or 1950s, local politicians also have a keen sense that Latinos have not yet coalesced into a political force that requires immediate attention.

Such attitudes provide some important insights into a larger set of popular American notions about the workings of politics and political systems. The debates raging over affirmative action and multiculturalism provide a barometer of the extent to which Americans currently disagree about the role that ethnic and other group affiliations should play in political organization and activism, but until fairly recently there seemed to be at least a working consensus that political conflicts between and among individual American citizens should be resolved by "working within the system." Whether the phrase was used to connote working through the electoral and representative mechanisms of the two-party system, or was more loosely applied to the jockeying for position of shifting political coalitions or formal and informally constituted "interest groups," "politics" in the United States has been construed as activity and mobilization that occurs within the bounds of the American constitutional system.

In general, Americans' assumptions about immigrants—and about the larger, transnational processes of immigration in which migrants move—have worked hand in glove with their larger beliefs about the workings of the political system. Indeed, in many ways, traditional American ideas about the "melting pot" and the gradual "assimilation" or "Americanization" of immigrants represented something of a continuation of their logic concerning politics in the national community. According to popular applications of this logic, immigrants are expected to follow a more or less linear path in their transformation from "foreigners" to "Americans." Thus, at the time of their initial entry into the United States, immigrants traditionally have been considered to be "outside" the political, social, and cultural community of the nation. Over time, however, permanent immigrants were expected to become Americans—to become integrated into the American polity and cultural community—by gradually shedding their former cultural and political affiliations and adopting American norms, especially (and at the very least) by learning English and ultimately naturalizing (Hirschman 1983; Kivisto 1990; Zunz 1985).

Of course, much of the current debate over immigration and immigration policy is drawn from this general conceptual and philosophical framework. Thus the presence of large numbers of foreign nationals—especially "illegal immigrants," who by popular understanding and juridical definition are outside the American political community—is generally portrayed as a deeply troubling anomaly fundamentally out of synch with popular understandings of how immigrants are supposed to behave and how they are supposed to fit into American society. Although specific attitudes about immigration may well run the gamut from the tempered phrasing of a moderate Democrat like Ted Kennedy to the racist, nativist tirades of white separatist or neo-Nazi groups, all positions can be said to derive in important ways from a more or less commonly held assumption: that immigrants (at least, "white" immigrants) should "become Americans" in the traditionally prescribed manner. By their very presence, "illegal aliens" have violated these expectations and thus are perceived as a serious threat to the established order.

This can be seen in any number of recent examples. Pat Buchanan (1994) views undocumented migrants as outlaws "who breach our borders and break our laws" and as cultural barbarians who threaten to overwhelm time-honored traditions of the "Americanization" and "assimilation" of immigrants to the United States. Centrist liberal California senator Dianne Feinstein has expressed more empathy toward economic immigrants than Buchanan, but she too has concluded that the influx of unsanctioned migrants "creates tension that is unhealthy to [American] society," and she has been an increasingly vocal spokesperson for immigration restriction (Rotella 1993: A3). Of course, having based his recent political comeback largely on the immigration issue, Pete Wilson has perhaps drawn the contours of the current debate in the clearest terms. For Wilson, the issue is unambiguous: undocumented migrants are lawbreakers who cannot be considered part of American society because they are "eroding the quality of life for legal residents of California. . . [and] threatening the quality of education that we can provide our children [and] the quality of care to our needy and blind, elderly and disabled" (Stall and McDonnell 1993: A12). From Wilson's perspective, boundaries must be maintained against the illegal immigrants who have been allowed to prey on "Californians who work hard, pay taxes, and obey the laws" (Weintraub 1994: A22).

Transnational Labor Migration Networks

The essential problem with this kind of formulation of the immigration issue and with similarly unexamined assumptions about the unambiguous and unitary nature of the modern United States is that they fly in the face of the complex countervailing reality that has evolved since World War II. However much Californians and other residents of the U.S.–Mexico border region would like to cling to the comforting notions of a clearly demarcated international border and a neatly bounded entity known as the United States of America, the increasing international economic, financial, and technology exchanges, instantaneous global communication and broadcast media networks, and deeply rooted transnational labor migration circuits and networks that have accompanied these trends have not only transformed the meanings of formal citizenship. They have also raised important questions about the nature of political community and, indeed, about the future of the nation-state itself (see Basch, Glick Schiller, and Szanton Blanc 1994; Soysal 1994; Rouse 1991, 1995).

It is perhaps precisely because these changes have evolved gradually over a long period that most Americans have failed to recognize their implications. But even a cursory review of the history of Mexican migration to the United States in this century reveals the extent to which, over the long run, American business practices, combined with U.S. immigration policies designed in large part to support those practices, helped to erode and eventually reconfigure the boundaries of the American national political community.

This process of reconfiguration began late in the nineteenth century as American capitalists began to lay plans for the economic development of Southern California and the rest of the southwestern United States. Compelled by the passage of the Chinese Exclusion Act of 1882 and the so-called Gentlemen's Agreement with Japan of 1908 to seek a new workforce to replace the Chinese and Japanese workers who had provided much of region's unskilled and semiskilled labor, employers increasingly looked to Mexico to meet this need (Cardoso 1980; Daniel 1981; Gutiérrez 1995). By the 1920s, after three decades of steadily increasing migration to the United States, Mexican workers had become the dominant source of labor in a broad range of industries, including agriculture, railroad construction and maintenance, and mining; they were also strongly represented in the canning, construction, steel, and auto manufacturing industries. From their employers' point of view, Mexicans constituted an ideal workforce because, as a U.S. government economist put it in 1908, they were "docile, patient, . . . orderly, . . . obedient, and cheap" (Clark 1908). In addition, employers used to great advantage the fact that

Mexican workers' status as noncitizens placed them in a particularly precarious legal position. The threat of deportation could be held over Mexicans seeking better wages, work hours, or working conditions. And when the U.S. economy experienced a recession (as in 1920–22) or an outright depression (as occurred on a massive scale during the Great Depression), Mexican workers—and their American-born children—could be expelled from the country with impunity (Carreras de Velasco 1974; Hoffman 1974; Balderrama and Rodríguez 1995).

But Mexican immigrant workers' ambiguous legal status could be manipulated in other, more subtle ways as well. For example, when nativists and immigration restrictionists began demanding the imposition of tighter controls on Mexican labor migration after World War I, southwestern employers' lobby groups responded by arguing that such controls were unnecessary since most Mexicans had no intention of remaining permanently in the United States. To the contrary, argued employers' spokesmen, Mexican workers had come merely to work and perhaps earn a small financial stake in the United States before happily returning to their homes in Mexico (Reisler 1976; Gutiérrez 1995).

Employers' experience in convincing Congress and the public about the benefits of using temporary Mexican labor between 1900 and 1929 was to serve them very well once the American economy recovered from the Great Depression. In early 1942, facing a severe and worsening shortage of labor caused by wartime conscription and the movement of American workers into defense jobs, regional employers immediately renewed their calls for the mass importation of "temporary" Mexican labor. Although the Mexican government refused to enter into any formal labor agreement with the U.S. government until it had won guarantees that Mexican nationals would receive fair wages, work hours, working conditions, and protection of their civil rights while working under contract in the United States, in many ways the Emergency Farm Labor Program (or, as it would soon become known, the "bracero program") tended to reinforce many of the same patterns of migration (and the abuse of migrant laborers) that had existed earlier in the century. The bracero program was officially announced as a temporary, emergency wartime measure; nevertheless, it was immediately renewed by Congress after the war's end and would be renewed under various guises for the next twenty-two years. At the program's peak in the 1959–1960 crop year, braceros represented fully 26 percent of the United States' agricultural labor force. By the time the foreign labor importation program was finally terminated in 1964, nearly five million bracero contracts had been issued.

The formal recruitment and employment of braceros tells only part of the story, however. For just as the first waves of migration north from Mexico at the turn of the century had helped to establish informal communication networks between Mexico and the United States (as Mexican workers moved back and forth between the two countries), the bracero program helped to establish extensive new lines of informal communication across the border. Gaining reliable information about labor market conditions from braceros returning periodically to Mexico after their contracts had expired, many Mexicans decided to chance crossing into the United States without the benefit of a formal contract.

Of course, since the presence of large numbers of undocumented (and legally unprotected) Mexican workers had the effect of driving wages down and undermining the efforts of U.S. farmworkers to organize for collective bargaining, many U.S. employers were delighted with the renewal of this trend in labor migration. As more and more Mexican workers surreptitiously passed into the United States in the late 1940s and early 1950s, the number of undocumented entries soon rivaled, and then exceeded, the number of braceros brought into the country under contract. Whereas the U.S. Immigration and Naturalization Service reported apprehending only about 159,000 undocumented Mexican workers per year in the mid-1940s, by the mid-1950s this number had jumped to more than 590,000 per year. It is estimated that over the life of the program, the number of undocumented workers who entered the United States outnumbered the formally contracted braceros by a ratio of at least four to one. In many ways, these patterns have persisted to the present day.[1]

Few Americans seemed to recognize it at the time, but the formal and informal encouragement of these kinds of migration patterns over many years inevitably transformed the social and cultural landscape of large parts of the United States. Just as many thousands of the earliest Mexican workers eventually decided to settle permanently in Mexican-American enclaves in the United States, many of those who came in the postwar era also eventually established permanent homes north of the border. In the process, Mexican immigrants (at first, predominantly single men; later, entire families) and their U.S.–born children helped to expand existing ethnic enclaves—in Los Angeles, Tucson, El Paso, San Antonio, and the lower Rio Grande Valley—or created new ones in the farmlands of the Pacific Northwest or the Great Lakes industrial belt.

Complete with a complex and growing infrastructure of small businesses, owner-occupied homes, Spanish-language churches, and diverse organizations and associations, the expansion of ethnic Mexican communities represented the development of a parallel society in

---

[1] On the long-term impact of the bracero program, see Calavita 1992; Cockcroft 1986; García y Griego 1983.

the United States. Of course, continuous exposure to elements of American popular and material culture powerfully influenced the evolution of these syncretic hybrid communities, but the continual influx of both permanent immigrants and sojourners from Mexico helped to sustain the distinctive cultural atmosphere of Mexican and Mexican American enclaves in cities, towns, and rural communities in the Southwest and Midwest.

The population data cited earlier in this paper underscore this point, but demographic figures reveal only the most superficial features of the changing social landscape. On a more submerged but no less significant level, the establishment of officially sanctioned and unsanctioned transnational migration circuits linking ethnic enclaves in the United States with communities in Mexico helped to disrupt traditional social relations in the United States by introducing a set of actors who didn't quite "fit" into the system of bounded categories Americans were used to. In other words, as the use of "temporary" foreign labor became a permanent feature of the American economy, the constant presence of a floating population of migrating workers began to strain a system long based on maintaining sharp distinctions between "natives" and "foreigners," "migrants" and "settlers," and, ultimately, "citizens" and "aliens." Indeed, over time, the establishment and maturation of transnational migration circuits linking communities in Mexico to ethnic Mexican enclaves in the United States produced several different kinds of communities among people who first crossed the border as part of these circulating streams.

Some migrants followed a path of incorporation that roughly mirrored the experiences of European immigrants to the United States. The growth of what some historians have called the "Mexican American generation" is emblematic of those who followed this path. While many of these individuals remained proud of their Mexican cultural heritage, they gradually made conscious decisions to distance themselves from that heritage and to emphasize what they perceived to be the "American" aspects of their social identities in their everyday lives. As one scholar described this process:

> Growing up in this country, [this group of] Mexican Americans [was] increasingly more acculturated, bilingual, and, as a result, more politically functional. Formally educated to a greater extent than ever before, they became better socialized to their rights as U.S. citizens. . . . For [these] Mexican Americans, there was no going back to Mexico. The United States was their home (García 1989: 15–6; see also Sánchez 1993).

Although such strategies may have fit nicely with mainstream expectations about how members of immigrant and ethnic groups should comport themselves once settled in the United States, strategies of accommodation and assimilation actually represented only one of a range of options that Spanish-speaking migrants adopted. Given the circumstances that Latino migrants faced in the United States, this is hardly surprising. Confronting severe obstacles to even the most basic levels of "assimilation" into American society, some migrants adapted in other ways.

Some were true sojourners who consciously entered the United States as a temporary expedient and did, in fact, eventually return permanently to Mexico. Considering themselves part of *México flotante* ("floating Mexico") or *México de afuera* (the expatriate community of Mexicans "outside of Mexico"), such individuals remained strongly oriented toward Mexico.

Another group chose to remain in the United States but made little or no effort to incorporate into the American polity. For these individuals, coping successfully in the United States did not necessitate their becoming "integrated" or "assimilated"—at least not in the manner most Americans would associate with these terms. Surrounded by people who generally spoke the same language, ate the same foods, enjoyed the same entertainments, celebrated the same holidays, and observed the same religious practices, these immigrants and at least some of their children carved out an intermediate social niche *between* the cultural communities of the United States and those of Mexico.

This is not to assert that these somewhat insular cultural enclaves were immune to the powerful influences of American consumer culture. On the contrary, constant participation in that culture of consumption deeply influenced immigrants and their U.S.–born children. Still, as recent research has amply demonstrated, the cultural exchanges that occurred in Mexican barrios as a result of this exposure was not a one-way, linear phenomenon. Rather, it was a process of continuous, and selective, engagement and appropriation in which settlers and sojourners operated in a social space between two or more cultural repertoires (see Peña 1985; Cohen 1990; Ruiz 1993; Sánchez 1993).

Over the past thirty years, yet another group—people who are part of various well-established transnational circuits—has become an increasingly important component of the Latino population residing in the United States. Fueled by the availability of comparably well-paying jobs north of the border and by a concomitant disruption of the economies of Mexico and other Latin American "sending" nations, labor flows across international frontiers have increased steadily since the end of the World War II. An essential difference in this flow, however, is that much more of it seems truly to circulate between locales in two (or even more) nation-states. Aided by the advent of cheap and fast air travel, instant communication systems, the means to transfer funds electronically, and the establishment of a vast network of Spanish-speaking communities north of the border, migrants can travel back and forth between communities in their natal countries and those in their "adopted" ones more easily than ever before. Indeed, some researchers have concluded that individuals involved in these circuits have become so habituated to this existence that they have largely ceased to think of themselves exclusively as members of this or that society or nation. As one group of researchers noted recently, "through their life ways and daily practices" migrants in these transnational streams have "reconfigure[d] space so that their lives are lived simultaneously within two or more nation-states" (Basch, Glick Schiller, and Szanton Blanc 1994: 28).

Political Implications

Traditional and deeply rooted ways of thinking about immigration and political identity have generally left Americans ill equipped to recognize the existence of these different kinds of migration experiences and communities. As a consequence, they have been even less able to recognize their important, even crucial, political implications for American society. Habituated to think in what can only be described as exclusive and ethnocentric terms about the superiority of the "American way of life," until recently few in the United States seemed to recognize that the continual recruitment and employment of large numbers of foreign workers over a very long period has inevitably—and irrevocably—changed American society. Thus, rather than acknowledging and attempting to deal constructively with the fact that a large, internally complex, growing Latino population is a *permanent* feature of regional and national life, most politicians and pundits continue to frame the issue in simplistic terms of "us" versus "them" and call for a series of draconian sanctions against noncitizen residents and their children who now live in the United States.[2]

The situation is complicated by the fact that, in many ways, Latinos seem to conform to the stereotypes that politicians and the media have exploited to frame the issue as a "crisis." Indeed, the very composition and internal characteristics of the Latino population in California make it fairly easy for unprincipled individuals to portray them as "outsiders." Although an increasing percentage of long-time Mexican American Californians have made significant strides in terms of socioeconomic mobility, levels of education, and general so-

---

[2] For very clear articulations of such views, see Gallegy 1996; Lacey 1996a, 1996b; and letters to editor, *Los Angeles Times*, May 13, 1996.

cial integration over the past three decades, when measured by in-
comes, occupational status, and levels of education, the Latino population in aggregate continues to occupy the very lowest rungs of the
economic system (Hayes-Bautista, Schink, and Chapa 1988: chaps. 4,
5; U.S. Bureau of the Census 1993: 18–22).

Largely as a consequence of these factors, Latinos have tended not
to participate in traditional forms of American political activity, all of
which tend to correlate positively with socioeconomic status, levels of
education, length of residence in the United States, and so on. In the
aggregate, Latinos register to vote in proportions far below those recorded for Anglo Americans. Moreover, Latinos—and particularly
ethnic Mexicans—historically have become naturalized U.S. citizens
at rates far below those recorded for other identifiable ethnic groups.
In 1982, for example, although more than 66 percent of resident European immigrants to California had become naturalized citizens, only
21 percent of eligible Latinos and 18.2 percent of Mexican residents
had become U.S. citizens, a pattern that has remained consistent over
a half-century. In the nation as a whole in the period 1976–1981,
Mexicans accounted for more than 13 percent of all immigrants to the
United States, and yet only 4.8 percent completed the naturalization
process (Hayes-Bautista, Schink, and Chapa 1988: chap. 7). More recently, although the passage of Proposition 187 has encouraged more
Latino legal residents to apply for U.S. citizenship, it is also likely that
the measure has discouraged other groups (particularly undocumented residents) from trying to regularize their status.

When adopting the vantage point of those who hold conventional
views of the American polity as one that is—or should be—defined
along strictly bounded lines demarcating "citizens" and "aliens," it is
not difficult to understand why many Californians and other Americans view the presence of a large and growing noncitizen population
as a serious political and cultural threat. From this perspective, the
illegal presence of such a large group of outsiders not only strains
limited resources but seems to contravene and undermine the very
meaning, value, and legitimacy of American citizenship (Schuck and
Smith 1985; Schuck 1989).

But adopting a broader perspective—one that takes into account
the experiences that Latino immigrants have lived and the different
kinds of communities they have built in the United States over the
past twenty-five or thirty years—leads one, at the very least, to question the continued utility of traditional ideas about the bounded nation-state that completely ignore such developments. Indeed, rather
than constantly trying to force a changing social reality to "fit" into
increasingly outmoded conceptual models of the nation and polity,
we might better rethink the criteria by which membership in our society is determined. Or, to borrow a phrase used in a different con-

text, it may be time for Americans to consider seriously the extent to which actual "social membership [in their society] entitles one to citizenship [in that society]" (Carens 1989: 32).

Although immigration restrictionists undoubtedly would protest this proposal, it may not be as radical as it first appears. At a very basic level, it merely calls on us to acknowledge the extent to which the kinds of economic and demographic shifts sketched above have rendered problematic the traditional American notions of community, polity, and nation. In other words, it is simply a call to reconcile the growing contradictions between our entrenched ideas about political, racial, and ethnic identities and a new reality that has tied the fate of "native" Californians to that of an increasingly complex amalgam of ethnic groups, "resident aliens," and habitual transnational border crossers.

How might such a change in orientation affect politics along the U.S.–Mexico border? On the most fundamental and perhaps most needed level, such a reorientation might allow Californians to begin to correct the myopia that has rendered Latinos invisible in this society. It is difficult to overstate the important trickle-down effects that such a change in perspective might generate. For example, if instead of denying the United States' role in the recruitment of "legal" and "illegal" labor, more political leaders framed the immigration debate by foregrounding the critical importance of the long history of foreign labor recruitment, the ad hoc and arbitrary nature of U.S. immigration law enforcement, and American consumers' tacit acceptance of these practices, it would become increasingly difficult to blame undocumented workers exclusively for the social strains and cultural tensions presently being experienced in California. Indeed, reframing the debate over immigration in this manner might help to alter public opinion on issues such as Proposition 187. An admission of even a modicum of our own responsibility in creating and helping to sustain conditions that have drawn migrant labor to the United States might expose such measures as not only unwise and shortsighted but perhaps criminally negligent as well.

This is not to assert that mere recognition of a permanent Latino presence in California will automatically mitigate the dangerous and increasing social and economic polarization that characterizes the border region. On the contrary, although a concerted public education campaign stressing the organic interconnectedness of the regional economy eventually might produce this outcome, it could well stimulate the opposite effect. As we have seen with the recent backlash against NAFTA, a suddenly heightened awareness of the transnational nature of the regional economy can also lead to demands that we turn back the clock by dismantling transnational relationships, militarizing the border, and reimposing strict legal distinctions between citizens and aliens on this side of the border.

On the other hand, there is some promising recent evidence that heightened awareness of the internationalization of the regional economy can lay the basis for American citizen workers to reassess their relationship to other workers within that economy. For example, various farm labor organizations have experimented with transnational organizing techniques for some time. More recently, some American labor, consumer, and environmental activists have taken the first tentative steps toward building bridges with workers in neighboring and even distant countries. Thus, although it may seem naive or even utopian to anticipate that American citizen workers might suddenly recognize a commonality of interest with noncitizen workers as both groups confront a similarly uncertain future in a steadily globalizing economy, one can at least imagine a scenario in which American workers might experiment with transnational coalition building as a matter of their own survival (see, for example, Aragón 1996; Arax 1996; Hayes-Bautista, Schink, and Chapa 1988: 145–50; Medina 1996; Rodríguez 1996).

Along a similar vein, recognizing the ongoing transnational reconfiguration of the border region might also provide a mechanism that would allow Latinos themselves to break out of the logjam that has snarled so much of their organized political activity in recent years. Although Latinos clearly have made significant strides in increasing their political visibility and voice over the past twenty years, in some crucial ways Latino political activists have been hampered by many of the same narrow assumptions that have constrained "mainstream" American politics. Given the limitations of most Latino activists' political horizons, this is hardly surprising. By adhering to traditional notions of citizenship and thus focusing almost exclusively on electoral politics, most mainstream Latino political leaders and organizations have, in effect, cut themselves off from thousands of noncitizen Latino residents. Just as the politics of citizenship in the mainstream political arena has tended to sharpen distinctions between an inner core of U.S. citizens and a marginalized group of noncitizens, who by definition are outside the political community of the nation, years of Latino participation in citizen-based politics has analogously tended to sharpen distinctions between citizens and aliens and other differences that traditionally have separated Latinos along national, class, generational, and regional lines. As the confused early responses to Proposition 187 amply demonstrated in 1993 and 1994, Latinos have too often reproduced the same kinds of invidious distinctions among themselves that they have struggled to eradicate in their dealings with the majority population. Whether based on derisive distinctions between citizens and aliens, natives and recent arrivals, *"pochos"* and "true Mexicans," or Chicanos and other Latinos, the effect of this internal sniping has been to waste energy and undermine effective political organization.[3]

I should make clear here that I am not predicting the imminent demise of either the nation-state or national politics based on formal notions of national citizenship. Nor would I argue that the internal identity politics that traditionally have divided Latinos is going to fade away. But I would argue that if current trends continue, and if history is any guide, large numbers of noncitizens will continue to play an important, perhaps crucial, role in the political economy of the border region and beyond. Given this fact, politically active Latinos would be well served by working to correct their own myopia about this issue, recognizing noncitizens as a crucial—and permanent—component of the resident population. In other words, it may well be time for Latinos to shed the conceptual blinders that have led many of them to dismiss noncitizens as politically irrelevant or, at the other extreme, to assume uncritically that Latino migrants necessarily have the same interests that U.S.–born Latinos do.

A more fruitful approach might be to change our orientation and embrace the complexities and ambiguities inherent in living in a transnational age rather than trying to maintain increasingly artificial distinctions between those of us who are "citizens" and those of us who are not. The potential benefits of recognizing strength in commonality rather than emphasizing difference in a locale such as San Diego County should be obvious. A region that percolates with daily transborder interactions and serves as a transition zone for migrants moving across the international frontier would seem ripe for the strategic building of coalitions between citizens and noncitizens.

Still, the shape that transnational politics would ultimately take in this scenario is an open question. As recent reactions to the passage of Proposition 187 have indicated, some transnational migrants undoubtedly will attempt to follow older methods for achieving political empowerment by entering the naturalization process (Ramos 1996). But there are historical precedents for the development of other possibilities as well. For example, at several points in this century regional transnational organizations—the Confederación de Uniones Obreras Mexicanas (CUOM) in the 1920s, El Congreso Nacional del Pueblo de Habla Española in the 1930s, the Asociación Nacional México-Americana (ANMA) in the 1950s, and El Centro de Acción Social Autónomo (CASA) in the 1970s—experimented with various types of partnerships between Latino citizens and noncitizens. The

---

[3] On this phenomenon, see Daley 1991; Gutiérrez 1995; Hayes-Bautista and Rodríguez 1996; Nazario 1996; Preciado and Burciaga 1991; Quintanilla 1995; Rodríguez 1996.

organizational ideologies, programmatic thrusts, and objectives of these coalition groups differed significantly, but they held in common a strong commitment to protecting and advancing, on an entirely equal basis, the rights of Latino workers in the United States regardless of their formal citizenship status. Although each of these organizations was short lived, their democratic experiments in coalition building both within and across ethnic, national, and international lines might well provide compelling models for Latino workers living in a transnational age.

References

Acevedo, Dolores, and Thomas J. Espenshade. 1992. "Implications of the North American Trade Agreement for Mexican Migration into the United States," *Population and Development Review* 18 (4): 729–44.

Aragón, Raymond G. 1996. "It's Time to Contain the Intolerance," *San Diego Union-Tribune*, April 12.

Arax, Mark. 1996. "The UFW Gets Back to Its Roots," *Los Angeles Times*, February 17.

Balderrama, Francisco E., and Raymond Rodríguez. 1995. *Decade of Betrayal: Mexican Repatriation in the 1930s*. Albuquerque: University of New Mexico Press.

Basch, Linda, Nina Glick Schiller, and Christine Szanton Blanc. 1994. *Nations Unbound: Transnational Projects, Postcolonial Predicaments and Deterritorialized Nation-States*. Basel, Switzerland: Gordon and Breach.

Bean, Frank D., and Marta Tienda. 1987. *The Hispanic Population of the United States*. New York: Russell Sage Foundation.

Bornemeier, James. 1993. "Boxer Urges Augmented Border Staff," *Los Angeles Times*, July 30.

Boswell, Thomas J. 1979. "The Growth and Proportional Distribution of the Mexican-Stock Population in the United States, 1910–1970," *Mississippi Geographer* 7: 57–76.

Braun, Stephen, and Sam Fulwood, III. 1996. "Buchanan Gets into Shouting Match over Immigration as Arizona Race Tightens," *Los Angeles Times*, February 24.

Buchanan, Patrick J. 1994. "Losing Control of America," *San Jose Mercury-News*, October 30.

Bunting, Glenn F. 1993. "Plan for National Guard at Border Gains Support," *Los Angeles Times*, October 19.

Bunting, Glenn F., and Alan C. Miller. 1993. "Feinstein Raises Immigration Profile," *Los Angeles Times*, July 18.

Calavita, Kitty. 1992. *Inside the State: The Bracero Program, Immigration, and the I.N.S.* New York: Routledge.

Cardoso, Lawrence A. 1980. *Mexican Emigration to the United States, 1897–1931*. Tucson: University of Arizona Press.

Carens, Joseph H. 1989. "Membership and Morality: Admission to Citizenship in Liberal Democratic States." In *Immigration and the Politics of Citi-*

zenship in Europe and North America, edited by William Rogers Brubaker. Lanham, Md.: University Press of America.

Carreras de Velasco, Mercedes. 1974. *Los mexicanos que devolvió la crises, 1929–1932*. México, D.F.: Secretaría de Relaciones Exteriores.

Clark, Victor S. 1908. *Mexican Labor in the United States*. Washington, D.C.: U.S. Department of Labor.

Cockcroft, James D. 1986. *Outlaws in the Promised Land: Mexican Immigrant Workers and America's Future*. New York: Grove.

Cohen, Lizabeth. 1990. *Making a New Deal: Industrial Workers in Chicago, 1919–1939*. New York: Cambridge University Press.

Corwin, Arthur F. 1978. "Quien Sabe? Mexican Migration Statistics." In *Immigrants—and Immigrants: Perspectives on Mexican Labor Migration to the United States*, edited by A. Corwin. Westport, Conn.: Greenwood.

Daley, Joe. 1991. "One Big Happy Family," *San Diego Reader*, May 6.

Daniel, Cletus. 1981. *Bitter Harvest: A History of California Farmworkers 1870–1941*. Ithaca, N.Y.: Cornell University Press.

Gallegy, Elton. 1996. "No 'Papers,' No School for Illegals," *Los Angeles Times*, May 14.

García, Mario T. 1989. *Mexican Americans: Leadership, Ideology, and Identity, 1930–1960*. New Haven, Conn.: Yale University Press.

García y Griego, Manuel. 1983. "The Importation of Mexican Contract Laborers to the United States, 1942–1964: Antecedents, Operation, and Legacy. In *The Border That Joins: Mexican Migrants and U.S. Responsibility*, edited by Peter G. Brown and Henry Shue. Totowa, N.J.: Rowman & Littlefield.

Goldman, Abigail, Eric Malnic, and Henry Weinstein. 1996. "Beatings Spur U.S. Investigation and National Debate," *Los Angeles Times*, April 3.

Gutiérrez, David G. 1995. *Walls and Mirrors: Mexican Americans, Mexican Immigrants, and the Politics of Ethnicity*. Berkeley: University of California Press.

———. 1996. "Myth and Myopia: Hispanic Peoples and Western History." In *The West: An Illustrated History*, edited by Dayton Duncan, Geoffrey Ward, and Stephen Ives. Boston: Little, Brown.

Hayes-Bautista, David E., and Gregory Rodríguez. 1996. "Winning More Political Offices but Still No Agenda," *Los Angeles Times*, February 11.

Hayes-Bautista, David E., Werner O. Schink, and Jorge Chapa. 1988. *The Burden of Support: Young Latinos in an Aging Society*. Stanford, Calif.: Stanford University Press.

Hernández Alvarez, José. 1966. "A Demographic Profile of the Mexican Immigration to the United States, 1910–1950," *Journal of Inter-American Studies* 8: 471–96.

Hirschman, Charles. 1983. "America's Melting-Pot Reconsidered," *Annual Review of Sociology* 9: 397–423.

Hoffman, Abraham. 1974. *Unwanted Mexican Americans in the Great Depression, Repatriation Pressures, 1929–1939*. Tucson: University of Arizona Press.

Kivisto, Peter. 1990. "The Transplanted Then and Now: The Reorientation of Immigration Studies from the Chicago School to the New Social History," *Ethnic and Racial Studies* 13 (4): 455–81.

Lacey, Mark. 1996a. "House GOP Immigration Plan Revised," *Los Angeles Times*, March 8.

———. 1996b. "Immigration Debate About to Resurface," *Los Angeles Times*, May 26.

Lorey, David E., ed. 1990. *United States–Mexico Border Statistics since 1900*. Los Angeles: Latin American Research Center, University of California, Los Angeles.

Martin, Philip, and Elizabeth Midgley. 1994. "Immigration to the United States: Journey to an Uncertain Destination," *Population Bulletin* 49 (2): 2–45.

Medina, Eliseo. 1996. "If We Don't Go Back to Grassroots Politics, We're in Trouble," *Los Angeles Times*, May 4.

Nazario, Sonia. 1996. "Natives, Newcomers at Odds in East L.A.," *Los Angeles Times*, March 3.

Peña, Manuel. 1985. *The Texas-Mexican Conjunto: History of a Working-Class Music*. Austin: University of Texas Press.

Preciado, Cecilia, and José Antonio Burciaga. 1991. "Prenuptial Jitters for Chicanos," *Los Angeles Times*, September 25.

Quintanilla, Michael. 1995. "The Great Divide," *Los Angeles Times*, November 17.

Ramos, George. 1996 "Latinos Push for Voters to Register," *Los Angeles Times*, June 1.

Reisler, Mark. 1976. *By the Sweat of Their Brow: Mexican Immigrant Labor in the United States, 1900–1940*. Westport, Conn.: Greenwood Press.

Rodríguez H., Javier. 1996. "A Challenge to Latinos," *Los Angeles Times*, April 4.

Rosenblatt, Robert A. 1996. "Latinos, Asians to Lead Rise in U.S. Population," *Los Angeles Times*, March 14: A1, A4.

Rotella, Sebastian. 1993. "Sen. Feinstein Gets Firsthand Look at Illegal Immigration," *Los Angeles Times*, July 9.

Rouse, Roger. 1991. "Mexican Migration and the Social Space of Postmodernism," *Diaspora* 1 (1): 8–23.

———. 1995. "Thinking through Transnationalism: Notes on the Cultural Politics of Class Relations in the Contemporary United States," *Public Culture* 7 (2): 353–402.

Ruiz, Vicki L. 1993. "'Star Struck': Acculturation, Adolescence, and the Mexican American Woman, 1920–1950." In *Building with Our Hands: New Directions in Chicana Studies*, edited by Adela de la Torre and Beatriz M. Pesquera. Berkeley: University of California Press.

Sánchez, George J. 1993. *Becoming Mexican American: Ethnicity, Culture, and Identity in Chicano Los Angeles, 1900–1945*. New York: Oxford University Press.

Sassen, Saskia. 1990. "U.S. Immigration Policy toward Mexico in a Global Economy," *Journal of International Affairs* 43 (2): 369–83.

Schuck, Peter H. 1989. "Membership and the Liberal Polity: The Devaluation of American Citizenship." In *Immigration and the Politics of Citizenship in Europe and North America*, edited by William Rogers Brubaker. Lanham, Md.: University Press of America.

Schuck, Peter H. and Rogers M. Smith. 1985. *Citizenship without Consent: Illegal Aliens in the American Polity.* New Haven, Conn.: Yale University Press.

Soysal, Yasemin Nuhoglu. 1994. *Limits of Citizenship: Migrants and Postnational Membership in Europe.* Chicago: University of Chicago Press.

Stall, Bill, and Patrick J. McDonnell. 1993. "Wilson Urges Stiff Penalties to Deter Illegal Immigrants," *Los Angeles Times*, August 8.

Thomas, David Hurst. 1991. "Harvesting Ramona's Garden: Life in California's Mythical Mission Past." In *Columbian Consequences: Vol. 3, Spanish Borderlands in Pan-American Perspective*, edited by D.H. Thomas. Washington, D.C.: Smithsonian Institution Press.

U.S. Bureau of the Census. 1991. *The Hispanic Population in the United States: March 1991.* Current Population Reports, Series P-20, No. 455. Washington, D.C.: U.S. Government Printing Office.

———. 1993. *Hispanic Americans Today.* Current Population Reports, P-23, No. 183. Washington, D.C.: U.S. Government Printing Office.

Weeks, John R., and Roberto Ham-Chande, eds. 1992. *Demographic Dynamics of the U.S.–Mexico Border.* El Paso: Texas Western Press.

Weintraub, Daniel M.. 1994. "Wilson Ad Sparks Charges of Immigrant-Bashing," *Los Angeles Times*, May 14.

Wilson, Pete. 1994. "Securing Our Nation's Borders," *Vital Speeches of the Day* 60 (17) (June 15): 534–36.

Zunz, Olivier. 1985. "American History and the Changing Meaning of Assimilation," *Journal of American Ethnic History* 5 (3): 53–84.

About the Contributors

RODOLFO O. DE LA GARZA is Mike Hoff Professor of Community Affairs at the University of Texas at Austin and Vice President of the Tomás Rivera Center. A leading expert on Latino politics, he is the author or editor of several publications, including *Barrio Ballots: Latino Politics in the 1990 Elections*; *The Mexican American Electorate: Political Participation and Ideology*; *Ignored Voices: Public Opinion Polls and the Latino Community*; and *The Mexican American Electorate: An Explanation of Their Opinions and Behavior*.

LEO F. ESTRADA is Associate Professor of Urban Planning in the School of Public Policy and Social Research at the University of California, Los Angeles. His areas of expertise include ethnic and racial demographic trends (particularly of the Latino population in the United States), inner-city redevelopment, social policy analysis, and research methods. Dr. Estrada has provided expert testimony on census undercount and redistricting issues.

PATRICIA GÁNDARA is Associate Professor in the Division of Education at the University of California, Davis. Her areas of research include educational reform and minority populations, Hispanic and bilingual education, and peer effects on educational achievement. She is the author of *Over the Ivy Walls: The Educational Mobility of Low-Income Chicanos*.

DAVID G. GUTIÉRREZ is Associate Professor of History at the University of California, San Diego. A specialist on Mexican American politics, immigration policy, and American civil rights history, he also worked briefly on the staffs of Congressman Edward R. Roybal and the Congressional Hispanic Caucus. He is the author of *Walls and Mir-*

rors: Mexican Americans, Mexican Immigrants, and the Politics of Ethnicity in the American Southwest, 1910–1986.

CAROLE J. UHLANER is Associate Professor of Politics and Society at the University of California, Irvine. Her main research area is comparative political behavior, with a focus on rational actor theories of political participation and the political experience of racial and ethnic groups in the United States, especially in California. Her research has been published in the *American Journal of Political Science, Political Behavior,* the *Journal of Politics,* and *Public Choice.* Dr. Uhlaner served on the advisory boards of the Latino National Political Survey and the Latino Political Ethnography Project.

ANÍBAL YÁÑEZ-CHÁVEZ is Assistant Professor of Geography in the Liberal Studies Program, an interdisciplinary unit at California State University, San Marcos. His teaching and research interests are in economic and regional geography, U.S.–Mexico border issues, and the spatial consequences of North American integration.